Python 2.7.10 Extending and Embedding Python

A catalogue record for this book is available from the Hong Kong Public Libraries.

Published in Hong Kong by Samurai Media Limited.

Email: info@samuraimedia.org

ISBN 978-988-8381-04-3

This document describes how to write modules in C or C++ to extend the Python interpreter with new modules. Those modules can not only define new functions but also new object types and their methods. The document also describes how to embed the Python interpreter in another application, for use as an extension language. Finally, it shows how to compile and link extension modules so that they can be loaded dynamically (at run time) into the interpreter, if the underlying operating system supports this feature.

This document assumes basic knowledge about Python. For an informal introduction to the language, see *tutorial-index*. *reference-index* gives a more formal definition of the language. *library-index* documents the existing object types, functions and modules (both built-in and written in Python) that give the language its wide application range.

For a detailed description of the whole Python/C API, see the separate *c-api-index*.

Note: This guide only covers the basic tools for creating extensions provided as part of this version of CPython. Third party tools may offer simpler alternatives. Refer to the binary extensions section in the Python Packaging User Guide for more information.

EXTENDING PYTHON WITH C OR C++

It is quite easy to add new built-in modules to Python, if you know how to program in C. Such *extension modules* can do two things that can't be done directly in Python: they can implement new built-in object types, and they can call C library functions and system calls.

To support extensions, the Python API (Application Programmers Interface) defines a set of functions, macros and variables that provide access to most aspects of the Python run-time system. The Python API is incorporated in a C source file by including the header `"Python.h"`.

The compilation of an extension module depends on its intended use as well as on your system setup; details are given in later chapters.

Note: The C extension interface is specific to CPython, and extension modules do not work on other Python implementations. In many cases, it is possible to avoid writing C extensions and preserve portability to other implementations. For example, if your use case is calling C library functions or system calls, you should consider using the `ctypes` module or the cffi library rather than writing custom C code. These modules let you write Python code to interface with C code and are more portable between implementations of Python than writing and compiling a C extension module.

1.1 A Simple Example

Let's create an extension module called `spam` (the favorite food of Monty Python fans...) and let's say we want to create a Python interface to the C library function `system()`. [1] This function takes a null-terminated character string as argument and returns an integer. We want this function to be callable from Python as follows:

```
>>> import spam
>>> status = spam.system("ls -l")
```

Begin by creating a file `spammodule.c`. (Historically, if a module is called `spam`, the C file containing its implementation is called `spammodule.c`; if the module name is very long, like `spammify`, the module name can be just `spammify.c`.)

The first line of our file can be:

```
#include <Python.h>
```

which pulls in the Python API (you can add a comment describing the purpose of the module and a copyright notice if you like).

Note: Since Python may define some pre-processor definitions which affect the standard headers on some systems, you *must* include `Python.h` before any standard headers are included.

---

[1] An interface for this function already exists in the standard module `os` — it was chosen as a simple and straightforward example.

All user-visible symbols defined by `Python.h` have a prefix of `Py` or `PY`, except those defined in standard header files. For convenience, and since they are used extensively by the Python interpreter, `"Python.h"` includes a few standard header files: `<stdio.h>`, `<string.h>`, `<errno.h>`, and `<stdlib.h>`. If the latter header file does not exist on your system, it declares the functions `malloc()`, `free()` and `realloc()` directly.

The next thing we add to our module file is the C function that will be called when the Python expression `spam.system(string)` is evaluated (we'll see shortly how it ends up being called):

```
static PyObject *
spam_system(PyObject *self, PyObject *args)
{
    const char *command;
    int sts;

    if (!PyArg_ParseTuple(args, "s", &command))
        return NULL;
    sts = system(command);
    return Py_BuildValue("i", sts);
}
```

There is a straightforward translation from the argument list in Python (for example, the single expression `"ls -l"`) to the arguments passed to the C function. The C function always has two arguments, conventionally named *self* and *args*.

For module functions, the *self* argument is *NULL* or a pointer selected while initializing the module (see `Py_InitModule4()`). For a method, it would point to the object instance.

The *args* argument will be a pointer to a Python tuple object containing the arguments. Each item of the tuple corresponds to an argument in the call's argument list. The arguments are Python objects — in order to do anything with them in our C function we have to convert them to C values. The function `PyArg_ParseTuple()` in the Python API checks the argument types and converts them to C values. It uses a template string to determine the required types of the arguments as well as the types of the C variables into which to store the converted values. More about this later.

`PyArg_ParseTuple()` returns true (nonzero) if all arguments have the right type and its components have been stored in the variables whose addresses are passed. It returns false (zero) if an invalid argument list was passed. In the latter case it also raises an appropriate exception so the calling function can return *NULL* immediately (as we saw in the example).

1.2 Intermezzo: Errors and Exceptions

An important convention throughout the Python interpreter is the following: when a function fails, it should set an exception condition and return an error value (usually a *NULL* pointer). Exceptions are stored in a static global variable inside the interpreter; if this variable is *NULL* no exception has occurred. A second global variable stores the "associated value" of the exception (the second argument to `raise`). A third variable contains the stack traceback in case the error originated in Python code. These three variables are the C equivalents of the Python variables `sys.exc_type`, `sys.exc_value` and `sys.exc_traceback` (see the section on module `sys` in the Python Library Reference). It is important to know about them to understand how errors are passed around.

The Python API defines a number of functions to set various types of exceptions.

The most common one is `PyErr_SetString()`. Its arguments are an exception object and a C string. The exception object is usually a predefined object like `PyExc_ZeroDivisionError`. The C string indicates the cause of the error and is converted to a Python string object and stored as the "associated value" of the exception.

Another useful function is `PyErr_SetFromErrno()`, which only takes an exception argument and constructs the associated value by inspection of the global variable `errno`. The most general function is `PyErr_SetObject()`, which takes two object arguments, the exception and its associated value. You don't need to `Py_INCREF()` the objects passed to any of these functions.

You can test non-destructively whether an exception has been set with `PyErr_Occurred()`. This returns the current exception object, or *NULL* if no exception has occurred. You normally don't need to call `PyErr_Occurred()` to see whether an error occurred in a function call, since you should be able to tell from the return value.

When a function *f* that calls another function *g* detects that the latter fails, *f* should itself return an error value (usually *NULL* or −1). It should *not* call one of the `PyErr_*()` functions — one has already been called by *g*. *f*'s caller is then supposed to also return an error indication to *its* caller, again *without* calling `PyErr_*()`, and so on — the most detailed cause of the error was already reported by the function that first detected it. Once the error reaches the Python interpreter's main loop, this aborts the currently executing Python code and tries to find an exception handler specified by the Python programmer.

(There are situations where a module can actually give a more detailed error message by calling another `PyErr_*()` function, and in such cases it is fine to do so. As a general rule, however, this is not necessary, and can cause information about the cause of the error to be lost: most operations can fail for a variety of reasons.)

To ignore an exception set by a function call that failed, the exception condition must be cleared explicitly by calling `PyErr_Clear()`. The only time C code should call `PyErr_Clear()` is if it doesn't want to pass the error on to the interpreter but wants to handle it completely by itself (possibly by trying something else, or pretending nothing went wrong).

Every failing `malloc()` call must be turned into an exception — the direct caller of `malloc()` (or `realloc()`) must call `PyErr_NoMemory()` and return a failure indicator itself. All the object-creating functions (for example, `PyInt_FromLong()`) already do this, so this note is only relevant to those who call `malloc()` directly.

Also note that, with the important exception of `PyArg_ParseTuple()` and friends, functions that return an integer status usually return a positive value or zero for success and −1 for failure, like Unix system calls.

Finally, be careful to clean up garbage (by making `Py_XDECREF()` or `Py_DECREF()` calls for objects you have already created) when you return an error indicator!

The choice of which exception to raise is entirely yours. There are predeclared C objects corresponding to all built-in Python exceptions, such as `PyExc_ZeroDivisionError`, which you can use directly. Of course, you should choose exceptions wisely — don't use `PyExc_TypeError` to mean that a file couldn't be opened (that should probably be `PyExc_IOError`). If something's wrong with the argument list, the `PyArg_ParseTuple()` function usually raises `PyExc_TypeError`. If you have an argument whose value must be in a particular range or must satisfy other conditions, `PyExc_ValueError` is appropriate.

You can also define a new exception that is unique to your module. For this, you usually declare a static object variable at the beginning of your file:

```
static PyObject *SpamError;
```

and initialize it in your module's initialization function (`initspam()`) with an exception object (leaving out the error checking for now):

```
PyMODINIT_FUNC
initspam(void)
{
    PyObject *m;

    m = Py_InitModule("spam", SpamMethods);
    if (m == NULL)
        return;

    SpamError = PyErr_NewException("spam.error", NULL, NULL);
    Py_INCREF(SpamError);
```

```
    PyModule_AddObject(m, "error", SpamError);
}
```

Note that the Python name for the exception object is `spam.error`. The `PyErr_NewException()` function may create a class with the base class being `Exception` (unless another class is passed in instead of *NULL*), described in *bltin-exceptions*.

Note also that the `SpamError` variable retains a reference to the newly created exception class; this is intentional! Since the exception could be removed from the module by external code, an owned reference to the class is needed to ensure that it will not be discarded, causing `SpamError` to become a dangling pointer. Should it become a dangling pointer, C code which raises the exception could cause a core dump or other unintended side effects.

We discuss the use of `PyMODINIT_FUNC` as a function return type later in this sample.

The `spam.error` exception can be raised in your extension module using a call to `PyErr_SetString()` as shown below:

```
static PyObject *
spam_system(PyObject *self, PyObject *args)
{
    const char *command;
    int sts;

    if (!PyArg_ParseTuple(args, "s", &command))
        return NULL;
    sts = system(command);
    if (sts < 0) {
        PyErr_SetString(SpamError, "System command failed");
        return NULL;
    }
    return PyLong_FromLong(sts);
}
```

1.3 Back to the Example

Going back to our example function, you should now be able to understand this statement:

```
if (!PyArg_ParseTuple(args, "s", &command))
    return NULL;
```

It returns *NULL* (the error indicator for functions returning object pointers) if an error is detected in the argument list, relying on the exception set by `PyArg_ParseTuple()`. Otherwise the string value of the argument has been copied to the local variable `command`. This is a pointer assignment and you are not supposed to modify the string to which it points (so in Standard C, the variable `command` should properly be declared as `const char *command`).

The next statement is a call to the Unix function `system()`, passing it the string we just got from `PyArg_ParseTuple()`:

```
sts = system(command);
```

Our `spam.system()` function must return the value of `sts` as a Python object. This is done using the function `Py_BuildValue()`, which is something like the inverse of `PyArg_ParseTuple()`: it takes a format string and an arbitrary number of C values, and returns a new Python object. More info on `Py_BuildValue()` is given later.

```
return Py_BuildValue("i", sts);
```

In this case, it will return an integer object. (Yes, even integers are objects on the heap in Python!)

If you have a C function that returns no useful argument (a function returning `void`), the corresponding Python function must return `None`. You need this idiom to do so (which is implemented by the `Py_RETURN_NONE` macro):

```
Py_INCREF(Py_None);
return Py_None;
```

`Py_None` is the C name for the special Python object `None`. It is a genuine Python object rather than a *NULL* pointer, which means "error" in most contexts, as we have seen.

1.4 The Module's Method Table and Initialization Function

I promised to show how `spam_system()` is called from Python programs. First, we need to list its name and address in a "method table":

```
static PyMethodDef SpamMethods[] = {
    ...
    {"system",  spam_system, METH_VARARGS,
     "Execute a shell command."},
    ...
    {NULL, NULL, 0, NULL}        /* Sentinel */
};
```

Note the third entry (`METH_VARARGS`). This is a flag telling the interpreter the calling convention to be used for the C function. It should normally always be `METH_VARARGS` or `METH_VARARGS | METH_KEYWORDS`; a value of `0` means that an obsolete variant of `PyArg_ParseTuple()` is used.

When using only `METH_VARARGS`, the function should expect the Python-level parameters to be passed in as a tuple acceptable for parsing via `PyArg_ParseTuple()`; more information on this function is provided below.

The `METH_KEYWORDS` bit may be set in the third field if keyword arguments should be passed to the function. In this case, the C function should accept a third `PyObject *` parameter which will be a dictionary of keywords. Use `PyArg_ParseTupleAndKeywords()` to parse the arguments to such a function.

The method table must be passed to the interpreter in the module's initialization function. The initialization function must be named `initname()`, where *name* is the name of the module, and should be the only non-`static` item defined in the module file:

```
PyMODINIT_FUNC
initspam(void)
{
    (void) Py_InitModule("spam", SpamMethods);
}
```

Note that PyMODINIT_FUNC declares the function as `void` return type, declares any special linkage declarations required by the platform, and for C++ declares the function as `extern "C"`.

When the Python program imports module `spam` for the first time, `initspam()` is called. (See below for comments about embedding Python.) It calls `Py_InitModule()`, which creates a "module object" (which is inserted in the dictionary `sys.modules` under the key `"spam"`), and inserts built-in function objects into the newly created module based upon the table (an array of `PyMethodDef` structures) that was passed as its second argument. `Py_InitModule()` returns a pointer to the module object that it creates (which is unused here). It may abort with a fatal error for certain errors, or return *NULL* if the module could not be initialized satisfactorily.

When embedding Python, the `initspam()` function is not called automatically unless there's an entry in the `_PyImport_Inittab` table. The easiest way to handle this is to statically initialize your statically-linked modules by directly calling `initspam()` after the call to `Py_Initialize()`:

```
int
main(int argc, char *argv[])
{
    /* Pass argv[0] to the Python interpreter */
    Py_SetProgramName(argv[0]);

    /* Initialize the Python interpreter.  Required. */
    Py_Initialize();

    /* Add a static module */
    initspam();

    ...
```

An example may be found in the file `Demo/embed/demo.c` in the Python source distribution.

Note: Removing entries from `sys.modules` or importing compiled modules into multiple interpreters within a process (or following a `fork()` without an intervening `exec()`) can create problems for some extension modules. Extension module authors should exercise caution when initializing internal data structures. Note also that the `reload()` function can be used with extension modules, and will call the module initialization function (`initspam()` in the example), but will not load the module again if it was loaded from a dynamically loadable object file (`.so` on Unix, `.dll` on Windows).

A more substantial example module is included in the Python source distribution as `Modules/xxmodule.c`. This file may be used as a template or simply read as an example.

1.5 Compilation and Linkage

There are two more things to do before you can use your new extension: compiling and linking it with the Python system. If you use dynamic loading, the details may depend on the style of dynamic loading your system uses; see the chapters about building extension modules (chapter *Building C and C++ Extensions with distutils*) and additional information that pertains only to building on Windows (chapter *Building C and C++ Extensions on Windows*) for more information about this.

If you can't use dynamic loading, or if you want to make your module a permanent part of the Python interpreter, you will have to change the configuration setup and rebuild the interpreter. Luckily, this is very simple on Unix: just place your file (`spammodule.c` for example) in the `Modules/` directory of an unpacked source distribution, add a line to the file `Modules/Setup.local` describing your file:

```
spam spammodule.o
```

and rebuild the interpreter by running **make** in the toplevel directory. You can also run **make** in the `Modules/` subdirectory, but then you must first rebuild `Makefile` there by running '**make** Makefile'. (This is necessary each time you change the `Setup` file.)

If your module requires additional libraries to link with, these can be listed on the line in the configuration file as well, for instance:

```
spam spammodule.o -lX11
```

1.6 Calling Python Functions from C

So far we have concentrated on making C functions callable from Python. The reverse is also useful: calling Python functions from C. This is especially the case for libraries that support so-called "callback" functions. If a C interface

---

makes use of callbacks, the equivalent Python often needs to provide a callback mechanism to the Python programmer; the implementation will require calling the Python callback functions from a C callback. Other uses are also imaginable.

Fortunately, the Python interpreter is easily called recursively, and there is a standard interface to call a Python function. (I won't dwell on how to call the Python parser with a particular string as input — if you're interested, have a look at the implementation of the `-c` command line option in `Modules/main.c` from the Python source code.)

Calling a Python function is easy. First, the Python program must somehow pass you the Python function object. You should provide a function (or some other interface) to do this. When this function is called, save a pointer to the Python function object (be careful to `Py_INCREF()` it!) in a global variable — or wherever you see fit. For example, the following function might be part of a module definition:

```
static PyObject *my_callback = NULL;

static PyObject *
my_set_callback(PyObject *dummy, PyObject *args)
{
    PyObject *result = NULL;
    PyObject *temp;

    if (PyArg_ParseTuple(args, "O:set_callback", &temp)) {
        if (!PyCallable_Check(temp)) {
            PyErr_SetString(PyExc_TypeError, "parameter must be callable");
            return NULL;
        }
        Py_XINCREF(temp);         /* Add a reference to new callback */
        Py_XDECREF(my_callback);  /* Dispose of previous callback */
        my_callback = temp;       /* Remember new callback */
        /* Boilerplate to return "None" */
        Py_INCREF(Py_None);
        result = Py_None;
    }
    return result;
}
```

This function must be registered with the interpreter using the `METH_VARARGS` flag; this is described in section *The Module's Method Table and Initialization Function*. The `PyArg_ParseTuple()` function and its arguments are documented in section *Extracting Parameters in Extension Functions*.

The macros `Py_XINCREF()` and `Py_XDECREF()` increment/decrement the reference count of an object and are safe in the presence of *NULL* pointers (but note that *temp* will not be *NULL* in this context). More info on them in section *Reference Counts*.

Later, when it is time to call the function, you call the C function `PyObject_CallObject()`. This function has two arguments, both pointers to arbitrary Python objects: the Python function, and the argument list. The argument list must always be a tuple object, whose length is the number of arguments. To call the Python function with no arguments, pass in NULL, or an empty tuple; to call it with one argument, pass a singleton tuple. `Py_BuildValue()` returns a tuple when its format string consists of zero or more format codes between parentheses. For example:

```
int arg;
PyObject *arglist;
PyObject *result;
...
arg = 123;
...
/* Time to call the callback */
```

```
arglist = Py_BuildValue("(i)", arg);
result = PyObject_CallObject(my_callback, arglist);
Py_DECREF(arglist);
```

`PyObject_CallObject()` returns a Python object pointer: this is the return value of the Python function. `PyObject_CallObject()` is "reference-count-neutral" with respect to its arguments. In the example a new tuple was created to serve as the argument list, which is `Py_DECREF()`-ed immediately after the `PyObject_CallObject()` call.

The return value of `PyObject_CallObject()` is "new": either it is a brand new object, or it is an existing object whose reference count has been incremented. So, unless you want to save it in a global variable, you should somehow `Py_DECREF()` the result, even (especially!) if you are not interested in its value.

Before you do this, however, it is important to check that the return value isn't *NULL*. If it is, the Python function terminated by raising an exception. If the C code that called `PyObject_CallObject()` is called from Python, it should now return an error indication to its Python caller, so the interpreter can print a stack trace, or the calling Python code can handle the exception. If this is not possible or desirable, the exception should be cleared by calling `PyErr_Clear()`. For example:

```
if (result == NULL)
    return NULL; /* Pass error back */
...use result...
Py_DECREF(result);
```

Depending on the desired interface to the Python callback function, you may also have to provide an argument list to `PyObject_CallObject()`. In some cases the argument list is also provided by the Python program, through the same interface that specified the callback function. It can then be saved and used in the same manner as the function object. In other cases, you may have to construct a new tuple to pass as the argument list. The simplest way to do this is to call `Py_BuildValue()`. For example, if you want to pass an integral event code, you might use the following code:

```
PyObject *arglist;
...
arglist = Py_BuildValue("(l)", eventcode);
result = PyObject_CallObject(my_callback, arglist);
Py_DECREF(arglist);
if (result == NULL)
    return NULL; /* Pass error back */
/* Here maybe use the result */
Py_DECREF(result);
```

Note the placement of `Py_DECREF(arglist)` immediately after the call, before the error check! Also note that strictly speaking this code is not complete: `Py_BuildValue()` may run out of memory, and this should be checked.

You may also call a function with keyword arguments by using `PyObject_Call()`, which supports arguments and keyword arguments. As in the above example, we use `Py_BuildValue()` to construct the dictionary.

```
PyObject *dict;
...
dict = Py_BuildValue("{s:i}", "name", val);
result = PyObject_Call(my_callback, NULL, dict);
Py_DECREF(dict);
if (result == NULL)
    return NULL; /* Pass error back */
/* Here maybe use the result */
Py_DECREF(result);
```

1.7 Extracting Parameters in Extension Functions

The `PyArg_ParseTuple()` function is declared as follows:

```
int PyArg_ParseTuple(PyObject *arg, char *format, ...);
```

The *arg* argument must be a tuple object containing an argument list passed from Python to a C function. The *format* argument must be a format string, whose syntax is explained in *arg-parsing* in the Python/C API Reference Manual. The remaining arguments must be addresses of variables whose type is determined by the format string.

Note that while `PyArg_ParseTuple()` checks that the Python arguments have the required types, it cannot check the validity of the addresses of C variables passed to the call: if you make mistakes there, your code will probably crash or at least overwrite random bits in memory. So be careful!

Note that any Python object references which are provided to the caller are *borrowed* references; do not decrement their reference count!

Some example calls:

```
int ok;
int i, j;
long k, l;
const char *s;
int size;

ok = PyArg_ParseTuple(args, "");  /* No arguments */
    /* Python call: f() */

ok = PyArg_ParseTuple(args, "s", &s);  /* A string */
    /* Possible Python call: f('whoops!') */

ok = PyArg_ParseTuple(args, "lls", &k, &l, &s);  /* Two longs and a string */
    /* Possible Python call: f(1, 2, 'three') */

ok = PyArg_ParseTuple(args, "(ii)s#", &i, &j, &s, &size);
    /* A pair of ints and a string, whose size is also returned */
    /* Possible Python call: f((1, 2), 'three') */

{
    const char *file;
    const char *mode = "r";
    int bufsize = 0;
    ok = PyArg_ParseTuple(args, "s|si", &file, &mode, &bufsize);
    /* A string, and optionally another string and an integer */
    /* Possible Python calls:
       f('spam')
       f('spam', 'w')
       f('spam', 'wb', 100000) */
}

{
    int left, top, right, bottom, h, v;
    ok = PyArg_ParseTuple(args, "((ii)(ii))(ii)",
            &left, &top, &right, &bottom, &h, &v);
    /* A rectangle and a point */
    /* Possible Python call:
       f(((0, 0), (400, 300)), (10, 10)) */
}
```

```
{
    Py_complex c;
    ok = PyArg_ParseTuple(args, "D:myfunction", &c);
    /* a complex, also providing a function name for errors */
    /* Possible Python call: myfunction(1+2j) */
}
```

1.8 Keyword Parameters for Extension Functions

The `PyArg_ParseTupleAndKeywords()` function is declared as follows:

```
int PyArg_ParseTupleAndKeywords(PyObject *arg, PyObject *kwdict,
                                char *format, char *kwlist[], ...);
```

The *arg* and *format* parameters are identical to those of the `PyArg_ParseTuple()` function. The *kwdict* parameter is the dictionary of keywords received as the third parameter from the Python runtime. The *kwlist* parameter is a *NULL*-terminated list of strings which identify the parameters; the names are matched with the type information from *format* from left to right. On success, `PyArg_ParseTupleAndKeywords()` returns true, otherwise it returns false and raises an appropriate exception.

Note: Nested tuples cannot be parsed when using keyword arguments! Keyword parameters passed in which are not present in the *kwlist* will cause `TypeError` to be raised.

Here is an example module which uses keywords, based on an example by Geoff Philbrick (philbrick@hks.com):

```
#include "Python.h"

static PyObject *
keywdarg_parrot(PyObject *self, PyObject *args, PyObject *keywds)
{
    int voltage;
    char *state = "a stiff";
    char *action = "voom";
    char *type = "Norwegian Blue";

    static char *kwlist[] = {"voltage", "state", "action", "type", NULL};

    if (!PyArg_ParseTupleAndKeywords(args, keywds, "i|sss", kwlist,
                                     &voltage, &state, &action, &type))
        return NULL;

    printf("-- This parrot wouldn't %s if you put %i Volts through it.\n",
           action, voltage);
    printf("-- Lovely plumage, the %s -- It's %s!\n", type, state);

    Py_INCREF(Py_None);

    return Py_None;
}

static PyMethodDef keywdarg_methods[] = {
    /* The cast of the function is necessary since PyCFunction values
     * only take two PyObject* parameters, and keywdarg_parrot() takes
     * three.
```

```
    */
    {"parrot", (PyCFunction)keywdarg_parrot, METH_VARARGS | METH_KEYWORDS,
     "Print a lovely skit to standard output."},
    {NULL, NULL, 0, NULL}   /* sentinel */
};

void
initkeywdarg(void)
{
    /* Create the module and add the functions */
    Py_InitModule("keywdarg", keywdarg_methods);
}
```

1.9 Building Arbitrary Values

This function is the counterpart to `PyArg_ParseTuple()`. It is declared as follows:

```
PyObject *Py_BuildValue(char *format, ...);
```

It recognizes a set of format units similar to the ones recognized by `PyArg_ParseTuple()`, but the arguments (which are input to the function, not output) must not be pointers, just values. It returns a new Python object, suitable for returning from a C function called from Python.

One difference with `PyArg_ParseTuple()`: while the latter requires its first argument to be a tuple (since Python argument lists are always represented as tuples internally), `Py_BuildValue()` does not always build a tuple. It builds a tuple only if its format string contains two or more format units. If the format string is empty, it returns `None`; if it contains exactly one format unit, it returns whatever object is described by that format unit. To force it to return a tuple of size 0 or one, parenthesize the format string.

Examples (to the left the call, to the right the resulting Python value):

```
Py_BuildValue("")                        None
Py_BuildValue("i", 123)                  123
Py_BuildValue("iii", 123, 456, 789)      (123, 456, 789)
Py_BuildValue("s", "hello")              'hello'
Py_BuildValue("ss", "hello", "world")    ('hello', 'world')
Py_BuildValue("s#", "hello", 4)          'hell'
Py_BuildValue("()")                      ()
Py_BuildValue("(i)", 123)                (123,)
Py_BuildValue("(ii)", 123, 456)          (123, 456)
Py_BuildValue("(i,i)", 123, 456)         (123, 456)
Py_BuildValue("[i,i]", 123, 456)         [123, 456]
Py_BuildValue("{s:i,s:i}",
              "abc", 123, "def", 456)    {'abc': 123, 'def': 456}
Py_BuildValue("((ii)(ii)) (ii)",
              1, 2, 3, 4, 5, 6)          (((1, 2), (3, 4)), (5, 6))
```

1.10 Reference Counts

In languages like C or C++, the programmer is responsible for dynamic allocation and deallocation of memory on the heap. In C, this is done using the functions `malloc()` and `free()`. In C++, the operators `new` and `delete` are used with essentially the same meaning and we'll restrict the following discussion to the C case.

Every block of memory allocated with `malloc()` should eventually be returned to the pool of available memory by exactly one call to `free()`. It is important to call `free()` at the right time. If a block's address is forgotten but `free()` is not called for it, the memory it occupies cannot be reused until the program terminates. This is called a *memory leak*. On the other hand, if a program calls `free()` for a block and then continues to use the block, it creates a conflict with re-use of the block through another `malloc()` call. This is called *using freed memory*. It has the same bad consequences as referencing uninitialized data — core dumps, wrong results, mysterious crashes.

Common causes of memory leaks are unusual paths through the code. For instance, a function may allocate a block of memory, do some calculation, and then free the block again. Now a change in the requirements for the function may add a test to the calculation that detects an error condition and can return prematurely from the function. It's easy to forget to free the allocated memory block when taking this premature exit, especially when it is added later to the code. Such leaks, once introduced, often go undetected for a long time: the error exit is taken only in a small fraction of all calls, and most modern machines have plenty of virtual memory, so the leak only becomes apparent in a long-running process that uses the leaking function frequently. Therefore, it's important to prevent leaks from happening by having a coding convention or strategy that minimizes this kind of errors.

Since Python makes heavy use of `malloc()` and `free()`, it needs a strategy to avoid memory leaks as well as the use of freed memory. The chosen method is called *reference counting*. The principle is simple: every object contains a counter, which is incremented when a reference to the object is stored somewhere, and which is decremented when a reference to it is deleted. When the counter reaches zero, the last reference to the object has been deleted and the object is freed.

An alternative strategy is called *automatic garbage collection*. (Sometimes, reference counting is also referred to as a garbage collection strategy, hence my use of "automatic" to distinguish the two.) The big advantage of automatic garbage collection is that the user doesn't need to call `free()` explicitly. (Another claimed advantage is an improvement in speed or memory usage — this is no hard fact however.) The disadvantage is that for C, there is no truly portable automatic garbage collector, while reference counting can be implemented portably (as long as the functions `malloc()` and `free()` are available — which the C Standard guarantees). Maybe some day a sufficiently portable automatic garbage collector will be available for C. Until then, we'll have to live with reference counts.

While Python uses the traditional reference counting implementation, it also offers a cycle detector that works to detect reference cycles. This allows applications to not worry about creating direct or indirect circular references; these are the weakness of garbage collection implemented using only reference counting. Reference cycles consist of objects which contain (possibly indirect) references to themselves, so that each object in the cycle has a reference count which is non-zero. Typical reference counting implementations are not able to reclaim the memory belonging to any objects in a reference cycle, or referenced from the objects in the cycle, even though there are no further references to the cycle itself.

The cycle detector is able to detect garbage cycles and can reclaim them so long as there are no finalizers implemented in Python (`__del__()` methods). When there are such finalizers, the detector exposes the cycles through the `gc` module (specifically, the `garbage` variable in that module). The `gc` module also exposes a way to run the detector (the `collect()` function), as well as configuration interfaces and the ability to disable the detector at runtime. The cycle detector is considered an optional component; though it is included by default, it can be disabled at build time using the `--without-cycle-gc` option to the **configure** script on Unix platforms (including Mac OS X) or by removing the definition of `WITH_CYCLE_GC` in the `pyconfig.h` header on other platforms. If the cycle detector is disabled in this way, the `gc` module will not be available.

1.10.1 Reference Counting in Python

There are two macros, `Py_INCREF(x)` and `Py_DECREF(x)`, which handle the incrementing and decrementing of the reference count. `Py_DECREF()` also frees the object when the count reaches zero. For flexibility, it doesn't call `free()` directly — rather, it makes a call through a function pointer in the object's *type object*. For this purpose (and others), every object also contains a pointer to its type object.

The big question now remains: when to use `Py_INCREF(x)` and `Py_DECREF(x)`? Let's first introduce some terms. Nobody "owns" an object; however, you can *own a reference* to an object. An object's reference count is now defined as the number of owned references to it. The owner of a reference is responsible for calling `Py_DECREF()` when the reference is no longer needed. Ownership of a reference can be transferred. There are three ways to dispose of an owned reference: pass it on, store it, or call `Py_DECREF()`. Forgetting to dispose of an owned reference creates a memory leak.

It is also possible to *borrow* [2] a reference to an object. The borrower of a reference should not call `Py_DECREF()`. The borrower must not hold on to the object longer than the owner from which it was borrowed. Using a borrowed reference after the owner has disposed of it risks using freed memory and should be avoided completely. [3]

The advantage of borrowing over owning a reference is that you don't need to take care of disposing of the reference on all possible paths through the code — in other words, with a borrowed reference you don't run the risk of leaking when a premature exit is taken. The disadvantage of borrowing over owning is that there are some subtle situations where in seemingly correct code a borrowed reference can be used after the owner from which it was borrowed has in fact disposed of it.

A borrowed reference can be changed into an owned reference by calling `Py_INCREF()`. This does not affect the status of the owner from which the reference was borrowed — it creates a new owned reference, and gives full owner responsibilities (the new owner must dispose of the reference properly, as well as the previous owner).

1.10.2 Ownership Rules

Whenever an object reference is passed into or out of a function, it is part of the function's interface specification whether ownership is transferred with the reference or not.

Most functions that return a reference to an object pass on ownership with the reference. In particular, all functions whose function it is to create a new object, such as `PyInt_FromLong()` and `Py_BuildValue()`, pass ownership to the receiver. Even if the object is not actually new, you still receive ownership of a new reference to that object. For instance, `PyInt_FromLong()` maintains a cache of popular values and can return a reference to a cached item.

Many functions that extract objects from other objects also transfer ownership with the reference, for instance `PyObject_GetAttrString()`. The picture is less clear, here, however, since a few common routines are exceptions: `PyTuple_GetItem()`, `PyList_GetItem()`, `PyDict_GetItem()`, and `PyDict_GetItemString()` all return references that you borrow from the tuple, list or dictionary.

The function `PyImport_AddModule()` also returns a borrowed reference, even though it may actually create the object it returns: this is possible because an owned reference to the object is stored in `sys.modules`.

When you pass an object reference into another function, in general, the function borrows the reference from you — if it needs to store it, it will use `Py_INCREF()` to become an independent owner. There are exactly two important exceptions to this rule: `PyTuple_SetItem()` and `PyList_SetItem()`. These functions take over ownership of the item passed to them — even if they fail! (Note that `PyDict_SetItem()` and friends don't take over ownership — they are "normal.")

When a C function is called from Python, it borrows references to its arguments from the caller. The caller owns a reference to the object, so the borrowed reference's lifetime is guaranteed until the function returns. Only when such a borrowed reference must be stored or passed on, it must be turned into an owned reference by calling `Py_INCREF()`.

The object reference returned from a C function that is called from Python must be an owned reference — ownership is transferred from the function to its caller.

1.10.3 Thin Ice

There are a few situations where seemingly harmless use of a borrowed reference can lead to problems. These all have to do with implicit invocations of the interpreter, which can cause the owner of a reference to dispose of it.

---

[2] The metaphor of "borrowing" a reference is not completely correct: the owner still has a copy of the reference.

[3] Checking that the reference count is at least 1 **does not work** — the reference count itself could be in freed memory and may thus be reused for another object!

The first and most important case to know about is using `Py_DECREF()` on an unrelated object while borrowing a reference to a list item. For instance:

```
void
bug(PyObject *list)
{
    PyObject *item = PyList_GetItem(list, 0);

    PyList_SetItem(list, 1, PyInt_FromLong(0L));
    PyObject_Print(item, stdout, 0); /* BUG! */
}
```

This function first borrows a reference to `list[0]`, then replaces `list[1]` with the value 0, and finally prints the borrowed reference. Looks harmless, right? But it's not!

Let's follow the control flow into `PyList_SetItem()`. The list owns references to all its items, so when item 1 is replaced, it has to dispose of the original item 1. Now let's suppose the original item 1 was an instance of a user-defined class, and let's further suppose that the class defined a `__del__()` method. If this class instance has a reference count of 1, disposing of it will call its `__del__()` method.

Since it is written in Python, the `__del__()` method can execute arbitrary Python code. Could it perhaps do something to invalidate the reference to `item` in `bug()`? You bet! Assuming that the list passed into `bug()` is accessible to the `__del__()` method, it could execute a statement to the effect of `del list[0]`, and assuming this was the last reference to that object, it would free the memory associated with it, thereby invalidating `item`.

The solution, once you know the source of the problem, is easy: temporarily increment the reference count. The correct version of the function reads:

```
void
no_bug(PyObject *list)
{
    PyObject *item = PyList_GetItem(list, 0);

    Py_INCREF(item);
    PyList_SetItem(list, 1, PyInt_FromLong(0L));
    PyObject_Print(item, stdout, 0);
    Py_DECREF(item);
}
```

This is a true story. An older version of Python contained variants of this bug and someone spent a considerable amount of time in a C debugger to figure out why his `__del__()` methods would fail...

The second case of problems with a borrowed reference is a variant involving threads. Normally, multiple threads in the Python interpreter can't get in each other's way, because there is a global lock protecting Python's entire object space. However, it is possible to temporarily release this lock using the macro `Py_BEGIN_ALLOW_THREADS`, and to re-acquire it using `Py_END_ALLOW_THREADS`. This is common around blocking I/O calls, to let other threads use the processor while waiting for the I/O to complete. Obviously, the following function has the same problem as the previous one:

```
void
bug(PyObject *list)
{
    PyObject *item = PyList_GetItem(list, 0);
    Py_BEGIN_ALLOW_THREADS
    ...some blocking I/O call...
    Py_END_ALLOW_THREADS
    PyObject_Print(item, stdout, 0); /* BUG! */
}
```

1.10.4 NULL Pointers

In general, functions that take object references as arguments do not expect you to pass them *NULL* pointers, and will dump core (or cause later core dumps) if you do so. Functions that return object references generally return *NULL* only to indicate that an exception occurred. The reason for not testing for *NULL* arguments is that functions often pass the objects they receive on to other function — if each function were to test for *NULL*, there would be a lot of redundant tests and the code would run more slowly.

It is better to test for *NULL* only at the "source:" when a pointer that may be *NULL* is received, for example, from `malloc()` or from a function that may raise an exception.

The macros `Py_INCREF()` and `Py_DECREF()` do not check for *NULL* pointers — however, their variants `Py_XINCREF()` and `Py_XDECREF()` do.

The macros for checking for a particular object type (`Pytype_Check()`) don't check for *NULL* pointers — again, there is much code that calls several of these in a row to test an object against various different expected types, and this would generate redundant tests. There are no variants with *NULL* checking.

The C function calling mechanism guarantees that the argument list passed to C functions (`args` in the examples) is never *NULL* — in fact it guarantees that it is always a tuple. [4]

It is a severe error to ever let a *NULL* pointer "escape" to the Python user.

1.11 Writing Extensions in C++

It is possible to write extension modules in C++. Some restrictions apply. If the main program (the Python interpreter) is compiled and linked by the C compiler, global or static objects with constructors cannot be used. This is not a problem if the main program is linked by the C++ compiler. Functions that will be called by the Python interpreter (in particular, module initialization functions) have to be declared using `extern "C"`. It is unnecessary to enclose the Python header files in `extern "C" {...}` — they use this form already if the symbol `__cplusplus` is defined (all recent C++ compilers define this symbol).

1.12 Providing a C API for an Extension Module

Many extension modules just provide new functions and types to be used from Python, but sometimes the code in an extension module can be useful for other extension modules. For example, an extension module could implement a type "collection" which works like lists without order. Just like the standard Python list type has a C API which permits extension modules to create and manipulate lists, this new collection type should have a set of C functions for direct manipulation from other extension modules.

At first sight this seems easy: just write the functions (without declaring them `static`, of course), provide an appropriate header file, and document the C API. And in fact this would work if all extension modules were always linked statically with the Python interpreter. When modules are used as shared libraries, however, the symbols defined in one module may not be visible to another module. The details of visibility depend on the operating system; some systems use one global namespace for the Python interpreter and all extension modules (Windows, for example), whereas others require an explicit list of imported symbols at module link time (AIX is one example), or offer a choice of different strategies (most Unices). And even if symbols are globally visible, the module whose functions one wishes to call might not have been loaded yet!

Portability therefore requires not to make any assumptions about symbol visibility. This means that all symbols in extension modules should be declared `static`, except for the module's initialization function, in order to avoid name clashes with other extension modules (as discussed in section *The Module's Method Table and Initialization Function*). And it means that symbols that *should* be accessible from other extension modules must be exported in a different way.

---

[4] These guarantees don't hold when you use the "old" style calling convention — this is still found in much existing code.

Python provides a special mechanism to pass C-level information (pointers) from one extension module to another one: Capsules. A Capsule is a Python data type which stores a pointer (void *). Capsules can only be created and accessed via their C API, but they can be passed around like any other Python object. In particular, they can be assigned to a name in an extension module's namespace. Other extension modules can then import this module, retrieve the value of this name, and then retrieve the pointer from the Capsule.

There are many ways in which Capsules can be used to export the C API of an extension module. Each function could get its own Capsule, or all C API pointers could be stored in an array whose address is published in a Capsule. And the various tasks of storing and retrieving the pointers can be distributed in different ways between the module providing the code and the client modules.

Whichever method you choose, it's important to name your Capsules properly. The function PyCapsule_New() takes a name parameter (const char *); you're permitted to pass in a *NULL* name, but we strongly encourage you to specify a name. Properly named Capsules provide a degree of runtime type-safety; there is no feasible way to tell one unnamed Capsule from another.

In particular, Capsules used to expose C APIs should be given a name following this convention:

```
modulename.attributename
```

The convenience function PyCapsule_Import() makes it easy to load a C API provided via a Capsule, but only if the Capsule's name matches this convention. This behavior gives C API users a high degree of certainty that the Capsule they load contains the correct C API.

The following example demonstrates an approach that puts most of the burden on the writer of the exporting module, which is appropriate for commonly used library modules. It stores all C API pointers (just one in the example!) in an array of void pointers which becomes the value of a Capsule. The header file corresponding to the module provides a macro that takes care of importing the module and retrieving its C API pointers; client modules only have to call this macro before accessing the C API.

The exporting module is a modification of the spam module from section *A Simple Example*. The function spam.system() does not call the C library function system() directly, but a function PySpam_System(), which would of course do something more complicated in reality (such as adding "spam" to every command). This function PySpam_System() is also exported to other extension modules.

The function PySpam_System() is a plain C function, declared static like everything else:

```
static int
PySpam_System(const char *command)
{
    return system(command);
}
```

The function spam_system() is modified in a trivial way:

```
static PyObject *
spam_system(PyObject *self, PyObject *args)
{
    const char *command;
    int sts;

    if (!PyArg_ParseTuple(args, "s", &command))
        return NULL;
    sts = PySpam_System(command);
    return Py_BuildValue("i", sts);
}
```

In the beginning of the module, right after the line

```
#include "Python.h"
```

two more lines must be added:

```
#define SPAM_MODULE
#include "spammodule.h"
```

The #define is used to tell the header file that it is being included in the exporting module, not a client module. Finally, the module's initialization function must take care of initializing the C API pointer array:

```
PyMODINIT_FUNC
initspam(void)
{
    PyObject *m;
    static void *PySpam_API[PySpam_API_pointers];
    PyObject *c_api_object;

    m = Py_InitModule("spam", SpamMethods);
    if (m == NULL)
        return;

    /* Initialize the C API pointer array */
    PySpam_API[PySpam_System_NUM] = (void *)PySpam_System;

    /* Create a Capsule containing the API pointer array's address */
    c_api_object = PyCapsule_New((void *)PySpam_API, "spam._C_API", NULL);

    if (c_api_object != NULL)
        PyModule_AddObject(m, "_C_API", c_api_object);
}
```

Note that PySpam_API is declared static; otherwise the pointer array would disappear when initspam() terminates!

The bulk of the work is in the header file spammodule.h, which looks like this:

```
#ifndef Py_SPAMMODULE_H
#define Py_SPAMMODULE_H
#ifdef __cplusplus
extern "C" {
#endif

/* Header file for spammodule */

/* C API functions */
#define PySpam_System_NUM 0
#define PySpam_System_RETURN int
#define PySpam_System_PROTO (const char *command)

/* Total number of C API pointers */
#define PySpam_API_pointers 1


#ifdef SPAM_MODULE
/* This section is used when compiling spammodule.c */

static PySpam_System_RETURN PySpam_System PySpam_System_PROTO;

#else
```

```
/* This section is used in modules that use spammodule's API */

static void **PySpam_API;

#define PySpam_System \
 (*(PySpam_System_RETURN (*)PySpam_System_PROTO) PySpam_API[PySpam_System_NUM])

/* Return -1 on error, 0 on success.
 * PyCapsule_Import will set an exception if there's an error.
 */
static int
import_spam(void)
{
    PySpam_API = (void **)PyCapsule_Import("spam._C_API", 0);
    return (PySpam_API != NULL) ? 0 : -1;
}


#endif

#ifdef __cplusplus
}
#endif

#endif /* !defined(Py_SPAMMODULE_H) */
```

All that a client module must do in order to have access to the function PySpam_System() is to call the function (or rather macro) import_spam() in its initialization function:

```
PyMODINIT_FUNC
initclient(void)
{
    PyObject *m;

    m = Py_InitModule("client", ClientMethods);
    if (m == NULL)
        return;
    if (import_spam() < 0)
        return;
    /* additional initialization can happen here */
}
```

The main disadvantage of this approach is that the file spammodule.h is rather complicated. However, the basic structure is the same for each function that is exported, so it has to be learned only once.

Finally it should be mentioned that Capsules offer additional functionality, which is especially useful for memory allocation and deallocation of the pointer stored in a Capsule. The details are described in the Python/C API Reference Manual in the section *capsules* and in the implementation of Capsules (files Include/pycapsule.h and Objects/pycapsule.c in the Python source code distribution).

DEFINING NEW TYPES

As mentioned in the last chapter, Python allows the writer of an extension module to define new types that can be manipulated from Python code, much like strings and lists in core Python.

This is not hard; the code for all extension types follows a pattern, but there are some details that you need to understand before you can get started.

Note: The way new types are defined changed dramatically (and for the better) in Python 2.2. This document documents how to define new types for Python 2.2 and later. If you need to support older versions of Python, you will need to refer to older versions of this documentation.

2.1 The Basics

The Python runtime sees all Python objects as variables of type PyObject*. A PyObject is not a very magnificent object - it just contains the refcount and a pointer to the object's "type object". This is where the action is; the type object determines which (C) functions get called when, for instance, an attribute gets looked up on an object or it is multiplied by another object. These C functions are called "type methods".

So, if you want to define a new object type, you need to create a new type object.

This sort of thing can only be explained by example, so here's a minimal, but complete, module that defines a new type:

```c
#include <Python.h>

typedef struct {
    PyObject_HEAD
    /* Type-specific fields go here. */
} noddy_NoddyObject;

static PyTypeObject noddy_NoddyType = {
    PyObject_HEAD_INIT(NULL)
    0,                      /*ob_size*/
    "noddy.Noddy",          /*tp_name*/
    sizeof(noddy_NoddyObject), /*tp_basicsize*/
    0,                      /*tp_itemsize*/
    0,                      /*tp_dealloc*/
    0,                      /*tp_print*/
    0,                      /*tp_getattr*/
    0,                      /*tp_setattr*/
    0,                      /*tp_compare*/
    0,                      /*tp_repr*/
```

```
    0,                        /*tp_as_number*/
    0,                        /*tp_as_sequence*/
    0,                        /*tp_as_mapping*/
    0,                        /*tp_hash */
    0,                        /*tp_call*/
    0,                        /*tp_str*/
    0,                        /*tp_getattro*/
    0,                        /*tp_setattro*/
    0,                        /*tp_as_buffer*/
    Py_TPFLAGS_DEFAULT,       /*tp_flags*/
    "Noddy objects",          /* tp_doc */
};

static PyMethodDef noddy_methods[] = {
    {NULL}  /* Sentinel */
};

#ifndef PyMODINIT_FUNC          /* declarations for DLL import/export */
#define PyMODINIT_FUNC void
#endif
PyMODINIT_FUNC
initnoddy(void)
{
    PyObject* m;

    noddy_NoddyType.tp_new = PyType_GenericNew;
    if (PyType_Ready(&noddy_NoddyType) < 0)
        return;

    m = Py_InitModule3("noddy", noddy_methods,
                       "Example module that creates an extension type.");

    Py_INCREF(&noddy_NoddyType);
    PyModule_AddObject(m, "Noddy", (PyObject *)&noddy_NoddyType);
}
```

Now that's quite a bit to take in at once, but hopefully bits will seem familiar from the last chapter.

The first bit that will be new is:

```
typedef struct {
    PyObject_HEAD
} noddy_NoddyObject;
```

This is what a Noddy object will contain—in this case, nothing more than every Python object contains, namely a refcount and a pointer to a type object. These are the fields the PyObject_HEAD macro brings in. The reason for the macro is to standardize the layout and to enable special debugging fields in debug builds. Note that there is no semicolon after the PyObject_HEAD macro; one is included in the macro definition. Be wary of adding one by accident; it's easy to do from habit, and your compiler might not complain, but someone else's probably will! (On Windows, MSVC is known to call this an error and refuse to compile the code.)

For contrast, let's take a look at the corresponding definition for standard Python integers:

```
typedef struct {
    PyObject_HEAD
    long ob_ival;
} PyIntObject;
```

Moving on, we come to the crunch — the type object.

```c
static PyTypeObject noddy_NoddyType = {
    PyObject_HEAD_INIT(NULL)
    0,                          /*ob_size*/
    "noddy.Noddy",              /*tp_name*/
    sizeof(noddy_NoddyObject),  /*tp_basicsize*/
    0,                          /*tp_itemsize*/
    0,                          /*tp_dealloc*/
    0,                          /*tp_print*/
    0,                          /*tp_getattr*/
    0,                          /*tp_setattr*/
    0,                          /*tp_compare*/
    0,                          /*tp_repr*/
    0,                          /*tp_as_number*/
    0,                          /*tp_as_sequence*/
    0,                          /*tp_as_mapping*/
    0,                          /*tp_hash */
    0,                          /*tp_call*/
    0,                          /*tp_str*/
    0,                          /*tp_getattro*/
    0,                          /*tp_setattro*/
    0,                          /*tp_as_buffer*/
    Py_TPFLAGS_DEFAULT,         /*tp_flags*/
    "Noddy objects",            /* tp_doc */
};
```

Now if you go and look up the definition of `PyTypeObject` in `object.h` you'll see that it has many more fields that the definition above. The remaining fields will be filled with zeros by the C compiler, and it's common practice to not specify them explicitly unless you need them.

This is so important that we're going to pick the top of it apart still further:

```c
PyObject_HEAD_INIT(NULL)
```

This line is a bit of a wart; what we'd like to write is:

```c
PyObject_HEAD_INIT(&PyType_Type)
```

as the type of a type object is "type", but this isn't strictly conforming C and some compilers complain. Fortunately, this member will be filled in for us by `PyType_Ready()`.

```c
0,                          /* ob_size */
```

The `ob_size` field of the header is not used; its presence in the type structure is a historical artifact that is maintained for binary compatibility with extension modules compiled for older versions of Python. Always set this field to zero.

```c
"noddy.Noddy",              /* tp_name */
```

The name of our type. This will appear in the default textual representation of our objects and in some error messages, for example:

```
>>> "" + noddy.new_noddy()
Traceback (most recent call last):
  File "<stdin>", line 1, in ?
TypeError: cannot add type "noddy.Noddy" to string
```

Note that the name is a dotted name that includes both the module name and the name of the type within the module. The module in this case is `noddy` and the type is `Noddy`, so we set the type name to `noddy.Noddy`.

```c
sizeof(noddy_NoddyObject),  /* tp_basicsize */
```

This is so that Python knows how much memory to allocate when you call `PyObject_New()`.

Note: If you want your type to be subclassable from Python, and your type has the same `tp_basicsize` as its base type, you may have problems with multiple inheritance. A Python subclass of your type will have to list your type first in its `__bases__`, or else it will not be able to call your type's `__new__()` method without getting an error. You can avoid this problem by ensuring that your type has a larger value for `tp_basicsize` than its base type does. Most of the time, this will be true anyway, because either your base type will be `object`, or else you will be adding data members to your base type, and therefore increasing its size.

```
0,                          /* tp_itemsize */
```

This has to do with variable length objects like lists and strings. Ignore this for now.

Skipping a number of type methods that we don't provide, we set the class flags to `Py_TPFLAGS_DEFAULT`.

```
Py_TPFLAGS_DEFAULT,         /*tp_flags*/
```

All types should include this constant in their flags. It enables all of the members defined by the current version of Python.

We provide a doc string for the type in `tp_doc`.

```
"Noddy objects",            /* tp_doc */
```

Now we get into the type methods, the things that make your objects different from the others. We aren't going to implement any of these in this version of the module. We'll expand this example later to have more interesting behavior.

For now, all we want to be able to do is to create new `Noddy` objects. To enable object creation, we have to provide a `tp_new` implementation. In this case, we can just use the default implementation provided by the API function `PyType_GenericNew()`. We'd like to just assign this to the `tp_new` slot, but we can't, for portability sake, On some platforms or compilers, we can't statically initialize a structure member with a function defined in another C module, so, instead, we'll assign the `tp_new` slot in the module initialization function just before calling `PyType_Ready()`:

```
noddy_NoddyType.tp_new = PyType_GenericNew;
if (PyType_Ready(&noddy_NoddyType) < 0)
    return;
```

All the other type methods are *NULL*, so we'll go over them later — that's for a later section!

Everything else in the file should be familiar, except for some code in `initnoddy()`:

```
if (PyType_Ready(&noddy_NoddyType) < 0)
    return;
```

This initializes the `Noddy` type, filing in a number of members, including `ob_type` that we initially set to *NULL*.

```
PyModule_AddObject(m, "Noddy", (PyObject *)&noddy_NoddyType);
```

This adds the type to the module dictionary. This allows us to create `Noddy` instances by calling the `Noddy` class:

```
>>> import noddy
>>> mynoddy = noddy.Noddy()
```

That's it! All that remains is to build it; put the above code in a file called `noddy.c` and

```
from distutils.core import setup, Extension
setup(name="noddy", version="1.0",
      ext_modules=[Extension("noddy", ["noddy.c"])])
```

in a file called `setup.py`; then typing

```
$ python setup.py build
```

---

at a shell should produce a file `noddy.so` in a subdirectory; move to that directory and fire up Python — you should be able to `import noddy` and play around with Noddy objects.

That wasn't so hard, was it?

Of course, the current Noddy type is pretty uninteresting. It has no data and doesn't do anything. It can't even be subclassed.

2.1.1 Adding data and methods to the Basic example

Let's expend the basic example to add some data and methods. Let's also make the type usable as a base class. We'll create a new module, `noddy2` that adds these capabilities:

```c
#include <Python.h>
#include "structmember.h"

typedef struct {
    PyObject_HEAD
    PyObject *first; /* first name */
    PyObject *last;  /* last name */
    int number;
} Noddy;

static void
Noddy_dealloc(Noddy* self)
{
    Py_XDECREF(self->first);
    Py_XDECREF(self->last);
    self->ob_type->tp_free((PyObject*)self);
}

static PyObject *
Noddy_new(PyTypeObject *type, PyObject *args, PyObject *kwds)
{
    Noddy *self;

    self = (Noddy *)type->tp_alloc(type, 0);
    if (self != NULL) {
        self->first = PyString_FromString("");
        if (self->first == NULL)
          {
            Py_DECREF(self);
            return NULL;
          }

        self->last = PyString_FromString("");
        if (self->last == NULL)
          {
            Py_DECREF(self);
            return NULL;
          }

        self->number = 0;
    }
```

```
    return (PyObject *)self;
}

static int
Noddy_init(Noddy *self, PyObject *args, PyObject *kwds)
{
    PyObject *first=NULL, *last=NULL, *tmp;

    static char *kwlist[] = {"first", "last", "number", NULL};

    if (! PyArg_ParseTupleAndKeywords(args, kwds, "|OOi", kwlist,
                                      &first, &last,
                                      &self->number))
        return -1;

    if (first) {
        tmp = self->first;
        Py_INCREF(first);
        self->first = first;
        Py_XDECREF(tmp);
    }

    if (last) {
        tmp = self->last;
        Py_INCREF(last);
        self->last = last;
        Py_XDECREF(tmp);
    }

    return 0;
}


static PyMemberDef Noddy_members[] = {
    {"first", T_OBJECT_EX, offsetof(Noddy, first), 0,
     "first name"},
    {"last", T_OBJECT_EX, offsetof(Noddy, last), 0,
     "last name"},
    {"number", T_INT, offsetof(Noddy, number), 0,
     "noddy number"},
    {NULL}  /* Sentinel */
};

static PyObject *
Noddy_name(Noddy* self)
{
    static PyObject *format = NULL;
    PyObject *args, *result;

    if (format == NULL) {
        format = PyString_FromString("%s %s");
        if (format == NULL)
            return NULL;
    }
```

```
    if (self->first == NULL) {
        PyErr_SetString(PyExc_AttributeError, "first");
        return NULL;
    }

    if (self->last == NULL) {
        PyErr_SetString(PyExc_AttributeError, "last");
        return NULL;
    }

    args = Py_BuildValue("OO", self->first, self->last);
    if (args == NULL)
        return NULL;

    result = PyString_Format(format, args);
    Py_DECREF(args);

    return result;
}

static PyMethodDef Noddy_methods[] = {
    {"name", (PyCFunction)Noddy_name, METH_NOARGS,
     "Return the name, combining the first and last name"
    },
    {NULL}  /* Sentinel */
};

static PyTypeObject NoddyType = {
    PyObject_HEAD_INIT(NULL)
    0,                         /*ob_size*/
    "noddy.Noddy",             /*tp_name*/
    sizeof(Noddy),             /*tp_basicsize*/
    0,                         /*tp_itemsize*/
    (destructor)Noddy_dealloc, /*tp_dealloc*/
    0,                         /*tp_print*/
    0,                         /*tp_getattr*/
    0,                         /*tp_setattr*/
    0,                         /*tp_compare*/
    0,                         /*tp_repr*/
    0,                         /*tp_as_number*/
    0,                         /*tp_as_sequence*/
    0,                         /*tp_as_mapping*/
    0,                         /*tp_hash */
    0,                         /*tp_call*/
    0,                         /*tp_str*/
    0,                         /*tp_getattro*/
    0,                         /*tp_setattro*/
    0,                         /*tp_as_buffer*/
    Py_TPFLAGS_DEFAULT | Py_TPFLAGS_BASETYPE, /*tp_flags*/
    "Noddy objects",           /* tp_doc */
    0,                         /* tp_traverse */
    0,                         /* tp_clear */
    0,                         /* tp_richcompare */
```

```
        0,                                      /* tp_weaklistoffset */
        0,                                      /* tp_iter */
        0,                                      /* tp_iternext */
        Noddy_methods,              /* tp_methods */
        Noddy_members,              /* tp_members */
        0,                          /* tp_getset */
        0,                          /* tp_base */
        0,                          /* tp_dict */
        0,                          /* tp_descr_get */
        0,                          /* tp_descr_set */
        0,                          /* tp_dictoffset */
        (initproc)Noddy_init,       /* tp_init */
        0,                          /* tp_alloc */
        Noddy_new,                  /* tp_new */
};

static PyMethodDef module_methods[] = {
    {NULL}  /* Sentinel */
};

#ifndef PyMODINIT_FUNC          /* declarations for DLL import/export */
#define PyMODINIT_FUNC void
#endif
PyMODINIT_FUNC
initnoddy2(void)
{
    PyObject* m;

    if (PyType_Ready(&NoddyType) < 0)
        return;

    m = Py_InitModule3("noddy2", module_methods,
                       "Example module that creates an extension type.");

    if (m == NULL)
      return;

    Py_INCREF(&NoddyType);
    PyModule_AddObject(m, "Noddy", (PyObject *)&NoddyType);
}
```

This version of the module has a number of changes.

We've added an extra include:

```
#include <structmember.h>
```

This include provides declarations that we use to handle attributes, as described a bit later.

The name of the Noddy object structure has been shortened to Noddy. The type object name has been shortened to NoddyType.

The Noddy type now has three data attributes, *first*, *last*, and *number*. The *first* and *last* variables are Python strings containing first and last names. The *number* attribute is an integer.

The object structure is updated accordingly:

```
typedef struct {
    PyObject_HEAD
    PyObject *first;
    PyObject *last;
    int number;
} Noddy;
```

Because we now have data to manage, we have to be more careful about object allocation and deallocation. At a minimum, we need a deallocation method:

```
static void
Noddy_dealloc(Noddy* self)
{
    Py_XDECREF(self->first);
    Py_XDECREF(self->last);
    self->ob_type->tp_free((PyObject*)self);
}
```

which is assigned to the `tp_dealloc` member:

```
(destructor)Noddy_dealloc,    /*tp_dealloc*/
```

This method decrements the reference counts of the two Python attributes. We use `Py_XDECREF()` here because the `first` and `last` members could be *NULL*. It then calls the `tp_free` member of the object's type to free the object's memory. Note that the object's type might not be `NoddyType`, because the object may be an instance of a subclass.

We want to make sure that the first and last names are initialized to empty strings, so we provide a new method:

```
static PyObject *
Noddy_new(PyTypeObject *type, PyObject *args, PyObject *kwds)
{
    Noddy *self;

    self = (Noddy *)type->tp_alloc(type, 0);
    if (self != NULL) {
        self->first = PyString_FromString("");
        if (self->first == NULL)
          {
            Py_DECREF(self);
            return NULL;
          }

        self->last = PyString_FromString("");
        if (self->last == NULL)
          {
            Py_DECREF(self);
            return NULL;
          }

        self->number = 0;
    }

    return (PyObject *)self;
}
```

and install it in the `tp_new` member:

```
Noddy_new,                    /* tp_new */
```

The new member is responsible for creating (as opposed to initializing) objects of the type. It is exposed in Python as the __new__() method. See the paper titled "Unifying types and classes in Python" for a detailed discussion of the __new__() method. One reason to implement a new method is to assure the initial values of instance variables. In this case, we use the new method to make sure that the initial values of the members `first` and `last` are not *NULL*. If we didn't care whether the initial values were *NULL*, we could have used `PyType_GenericNew()` as our new method, as we did before. `PyType_GenericNew()` initializes all of the instance variable members to *NULL*.

The new method is a static method that is passed the type being instantiated and any arguments passed when the type was called, and that returns the new object created. New methods always accept positional and keyword arguments, but they often ignore the arguments, leaving the argument handling to initializer methods. Note that if the type supports subclassing, the type passed may not be the type being defined. The new method calls the tp_alloc slot to allocate memory. We don't fill the tp_alloc slot ourselves. Rather `PyType_Ready()` fills it for us by inheriting it from our base class, which is `object` by default. Most types use the default allocation.

Note: If you are creating a co-operative `tp_new` (one that calls a base type's `tp_new` or __new__()), you must *not* try to determine what method to call using method resolution order at runtime. Always statically determine what type you are going to call, and call its `tp_new` directly, or via `type->tp_base->tp_new`. If you do not do this, Python subclasses of your type that also inherit from other Python-defined classes may not work correctly. (Specifically, you may not be able to create instances of such subclasses without getting a `TypeError`.)

We provide an initialization function:

```c
static int
Noddy_init(Noddy *self, PyObject *args, PyObject *kwds)
{
    PyObject *first=NULL, *last=NULL, *tmp;

    static char *kwlist[] = {"first", "last", "number", NULL};

    if (! PyArg_ParseTupleAndKeywords(args, kwds, "|OOi", kwlist,
                                      &first, &last,
                                      &self->number))
        return -1;

    if (first) {
        tmp = self->first;
        Py_INCREF(first);
        self->first = first;
        Py_XDECREF(tmp);
    }

    if (last) {
        tmp = self->last;
        Py_INCREF(last);
        self->last = last;
        Py_XDECREF(tmp);
    }

    return 0;
}
```

by filling the `tp_init` slot.

```
(initproc)Noddy_init,         /* tp_init */
```

The `tp_init` slot is exposed in Python as the `__init__()` method. It is used to initialize an object after it's created. Unlike the new method, we can't guarantee that the initializer is called. The initializer isn't called when unpickling objects and it can be overridden. Our initializer accepts arguments to provide initial values for our instance. Initializers always accept positional and keyword arguments.

Initializers can be called multiple times. Anyone can call the `__init__()` method on our objects. For this reason, we have to be extra careful when assigning the new values. We might be tempted, for example to assign the `first` member like this:

```
if (first) {
    Py_XDECREF(self->first);
    Py_INCREF(first);
    self->first = first;
}
```

But this would be risky. Our type doesn't restrict the type of the `first` member, so it could be any kind of object. It could have a destructor that causes code to be executed that tries to access the `first` member. To be paranoid and protect ourselves against this possibility, we almost always reassign members before decrementing their reference counts. When don't we have to do this?

- when we absolutely know that the reference count is greater than 1

- when we know that deallocation of the object [1] will not cause any calls back into our type's code

- when decrementing a reference count in a `tp_dealloc` handler when garbage-collections is not supported [2]

We want to expose our instance variables as attributes. There are a number of ways to do that. The simplest way is to define member definitions:

```
static PyMemberDef Noddy_members[] = {
    {"first", T_OBJECT_EX, offsetof(Noddy, first), 0,
     "first name"},
    {"last", T_OBJECT_EX, offsetof(Noddy, last), 0,
     "last name"},
    {"number", T_INT, offsetof(Noddy, number), 0,
     "noddy number"},
    {NULL}  /* Sentinel */
};
```

and put the definitions in the `tp_members` slot:

```
Noddy_members,                  /* tp_members */
```

Each member definition has a member name, type, offset, access flags and documentation string. See the *Generic Attribute Management* section below for details.

A disadvantage of this approach is that it doesn't provide a way to restrict the types of objects that can be assigned to the Python attributes. We expect the first and last names to be strings, but any Python objects can be assigned. Further, the attributes can be deleted, setting the C pointers to *NULL*. Even though we can make sure the members are initialized to non-*NULL* values, the members can be set to *NULL* if the attributes are deleted.

We define a single method, `name()`, that outputs the objects name as the concatenation of the first and last names.

```
static PyObject *
Noddy_name(Noddy* self)
{
    static PyObject *format = NULL;
```

---

[1] This is true when we know that the object is a basic type, like a string or a float.

[2] We relied on this in the `tp_dealloc` handler in this example, because our type doesn't support garbage collection. Even if a type supports garbage collection, there are calls that can be made to "untrack" the object from garbage collection, however, these calls are advanced and not covered here.

```
    PyObject *args, *result;

    if (format == NULL) {
        format = PyString_FromString("%s %s");
        if (format == NULL)
            return NULL;
    }

    if (self->first == NULL) {
        PyErr_SetString(PyExc_AttributeError, "first");
        return NULL;
    }

    if (self->last == NULL) {
        PyErr_SetString(PyExc_AttributeError, "last");
        return NULL;
    }

    args = Py_BuildValue("OO", self->first, self->last);
    if (args == NULL)
        return NULL;

    result = PyString_Format(format, args);
    Py_DECREF(args);

    return result;
}
```

The method is implemented as a C function that takes a `Noddy` (or `Noddy` subclass) instance as the first argument. Methods always take an instance as the first argument. Methods often take positional and keyword arguments as well, but in this cased we don't take any and don't need to accept a positional argument tuple or keyword argument dictionary. This method is equivalent to the Python method:

```
def name(self):
    return "%s %s" % (self.first, self.last)
```

Note that we have to check for the possibility that our `first` and `last` members are *NULL*. This is because they can be deleted, in which case they are set to *NULL*. It would be better to prevent deletion of these attributes and to restrict the attribute values to be strings. We'll see how to do that in the next section.

Now that we've defined the method, we need to create an array of method definitions:

```
static PyMethodDef Noddy_methods[] = {
    {"name", (PyCFunction)Noddy_name, METH_NOARGS,
     "Return the name, combining the first and last name"
    },
    {NULL}  /* Sentinel */
};
```

and assign them to the `tp_methods` slot:

```
Noddy_methods,                  /* tp_methods */
```

Note that we used the `METH_NOARGS` flag to indicate that the method is passed no arguments.

Finally, we'll make our type usable as a base class. We've written our methods carefully so far so that they don't make any assumptions about the type of the object being created or used, so all we need to do is to add the `Py_TPFLAGS_BASETYPE` to our class flag definition:

```
Py_TPFLAGS_DEFAULT | Py_TPFLAGS_BASETYPE, /*tp_flags*/
```

We rename `initnoddy()` to `initnoddy2()` and update the module name passed to `Py_InitModule3()`.

Finally, we update our `setup.py` file to build the new module:

```python
from distutils.core import setup, Extension
setup(name="noddy", version="1.0",
      ext_modules=[
          Extension("noddy", ["noddy.c"]),
          Extension("noddy2", ["noddy2.c"]),
          ])
```

2.1.2 Providing finer control over data attributes

In this section, we'll provide finer control over how the `first` and `last` attributes are set in the Noddy example. In the previous version of our module, the instance variables `first` and `last` could be set to non-string values or even deleted. We want to make sure that these attributes always contain strings.

```c
#include <Python.h>
#include "structmember.h"

typedef struct {
    PyObject_HEAD
    PyObject *first;
    PyObject *last;
    int number;
} Noddy;

static void
Noddy_dealloc(Noddy* self)
{
    Py_XDECREF(self->first);
    Py_XDECREF(self->last);
    self->ob_type->tp_free((PyObject*)self);
}

static PyObject *
Noddy_new(PyTypeObject *type, PyObject *args, PyObject *kwds)
{
    Noddy *self;

    self = (Noddy *)type->tp_alloc(type, 0);
    if (self != NULL) {
        self->first = PyString_FromString("");
        if (self->first == NULL)
          {
            Py_DECREF(self);
            return NULL;
          }

        self->last = PyString_FromString("");
        if (self->last == NULL)
          {
            Py_DECREF(self);
```

```
            return NULL;
        }

        self->number = 0;
    }

    return (PyObject *)self;
}

static int
Noddy_init(Noddy *self, PyObject *args, PyObject *kwds)
{
    PyObject *first=NULL, *last=NULL, *tmp;

    static char *kwlist[] = {"first", "last", "number", NULL};

    if (! PyArg_ParseTupleAndKeywords(args, kwds, "|SSi", kwlist,
                                      &first, &last,
                                      &self->number))
        return -1;

    if (first) {
        tmp = self->first;
        Py_INCREF(first);
        self->first = first;
        Py_DECREF(tmp);
    }

    if (last) {
        tmp = self->last;
        Py_INCREF(last);
        self->last = last;
        Py_DECREF(tmp);
    }

    return 0;
}

static PyMemberDef Noddy_members[] = {
    {"number", T_INT, offsetof(Noddy, number), 0,
     "noddy number"},
    {NULL}  /* Sentinel */
};

static PyObject *
Noddy_getfirst(Noddy *self, void *closure)
{
    Py_INCREF(self->first);
    return self->first;
}

static int
Noddy_setfirst(Noddy *self, PyObject *value, void *closure)
{
```

```c
  if (value == NULL) {
    PyErr_SetString(PyExc_TypeError, "Cannot delete the first attribute");
    return -1;
  }

  if (! PyString_Check(value)) {
    PyErr_SetString(PyExc_TypeError,
                    "The first attribute value must be a string");
    return -1;
  }

  Py_DECREF(self->first);
  Py_INCREF(value);
  self->first = value;

  return 0;
}

static PyObject *
Noddy_getlast(Noddy *self, void *closure)
{
    Py_INCREF(self->last);
    return self->last;
}

static int
Noddy_setlast(Noddy *self, PyObject *value, void *closure)
{
  if (value == NULL) {
    PyErr_SetString(PyExc_TypeError, "Cannot delete the last attribute");
    return -1;
  }

  if (! PyString_Check(value)) {
    PyErr_SetString(PyExc_TypeError,
                    "The last attribute value must be a string");
    return -1;
  }

  Py_DECREF(self->last);
  Py_INCREF(value);
  self->last = value;

  return 0;
}

static PyGetSetDef Noddy_getseters[] = {
    {"first",
     (getter)Noddy_getfirst, (setter)Noddy_setfirst,
     "first name",
     NULL},
    {"last",
     (getter)Noddy_getlast, (setter)Noddy_setlast,
     "last name",
```

```
    NULL},
    {NULL}  /* Sentinel */
};

static PyObject *
Noddy_name(Noddy* self)
{
    static PyObject *format = NULL;
    PyObject *args, *result;

    if (format == NULL) {
        format = PyString_FromString("%s %s");
        if (format == NULL)
            return NULL;
    }

    args = Py_BuildValue("OO", self->first, self->last);
    if (args == NULL)
        return NULL;

    result = PyString_Format(format, args);
    Py_DECREF(args);

    return result;
}

static PyMethodDef Noddy_methods[] = {
    {"name", (PyCFunction)Noddy_name, METH_NOARGS,
     "Return the name, combining the first and last name"
    },
    {NULL}  /* Sentinel */
};

static PyTypeObject NoddyType = {
    PyObject_HEAD_INIT(NULL)
    0,                         /*ob_size*/
    "noddy.Noddy",             /*tp_name*/
    sizeof(Noddy),             /*tp_basicsize*/
    0,                         /*tp_itemsize*/
    (destructor)Noddy_dealloc, /*tp_dealloc*/
    0,                         /*tp_print*/
    0,                         /*tp_getattr*/
    0,                         /*tp_setattr*/
    0,                         /*tp_compare*/
    0,                         /*tp_repr*/
    0,                         /*tp_as_number*/
    0,                         /*tp_as_sequence*/
    0,                         /*tp_as_mapping*/
    0,                         /*tp_hash */
    0,                         /*tp_call*/
    0,                         /*tp_str*/
    0,                         /*tp_getattro*/
    0,                         /*tp_setattro*/
    0,                         /*tp_as_buffer*/
```

```
    Py_TPFLAGS_DEFAULT | Py_TPFLAGS_BASETYPE, /*tp_flags*/
    "Noddy objects",           /* tp_doc */
    0,                                /* tp_traverse */
    0,                                /* tp_clear */
    0,                                /* tp_richcompare */
    0,                                /* tp_weaklistoffset */
    0,                                /* tp_iter */
    0,                                /* tp_iternext */
    Noddy_methods,             /* tp_methods */
    Noddy_members,             /* tp_members */
    Noddy_getseters,           /* tp_getset */
    0,                         /* tp_base */
    0,                         /* tp_dict */
    0,                         /* tp_descr_get */
    0,                         /* tp_descr_set */
    0,                         /* tp_dictoffset */
    (initproc)Noddy_init,      /* tp_init */
    0,                         /* tp_alloc */
    Noddy_new,                 /* tp_new */
};

static PyMethodDef module_methods[] = {
    {NULL}  /* Sentinel */
};

#ifndef PyMODINIT_FUNC          /* declarations for DLL import/export */
#define PyMODINIT_FUNC void
#endif
PyMODINIT_FUNC
initnoddy3(void)
{
    PyObject* m;

    if (PyType_Ready(&NoddyType) < 0)
        return;

    m = Py_InitModule3("noddy3", module_methods,
                       "Example module that creates an extension type.");

    if (m == NULL)
      return;

    Py_INCREF(&NoddyType);
    PyModule_AddObject(m, "Noddy", (PyObject *)&NoddyType);
}
```

To provide greater control, over the `first` and `last` attributes, we'll use custom getter and setter functions. Here are the functions for getting and setting the `first` attribute:

```
Noddy_getfirst(Noddy *self, void *closure)
{
    Py_INCREF(self->first);
    return self->first;
}
```

```
static int
Noddy_setfirst(Noddy *self, PyObject *value, void *closure)
{
  if (value == NULL) {
    PyErr_SetString(PyExc_TypeError, "Cannot delete the first attribute");
    return -1;
  }

  if (! PyString_Check(value)) {
    PyErr_SetString(PyExc_TypeError,
                    "The first attribute value must be a string");
    return -1;
  }

  Py_DECREF(self->first);
  Py_INCREF(value);
  self->first = value;

  return 0;
}
```

The getter function is passed a `Noddy` object and a "closure", which is void pointer. In this case, the closure is ignored. (The closure supports an advanced usage in which definition data is passed to the getter and setter. This could, for example, be used to allow a single set of getter and setter functions that decide the attribute to get or set based on data in the closure.)

The setter function is passed the `Noddy` object, the new value, and the closure. The new value may be *NULL*, in which case the attribute is being deleted. In our setter, we raise an error if the attribute is deleted or if the attribute value is not a string.

We create an array of `PyGetSetDef` structures:

```
static PyGetSetDef Noddy_getseters[] = {
    {"first",
     (getter)Noddy_getfirst, (setter)Noddy_setfirst,
     "first name",
     NULL},
    {"last",
     (getter)Noddy_getlast, (setter)Noddy_setlast,
     "last name",
     NULL},
    {NULL}  /* Sentinel */
};
```

and register it in the `tp_getset` slot:

```
Noddy_getseters,              /* tp_getset */
```

to register our attribute getters and setters.

The last item in a `PyGetSetDef` structure is the closure mentioned above. In this case, we aren't using the closure, so we just pass *NULL*.

We also remove the member definitions for these attributes:

```
static PyMemberDef Noddy_members[] = {
    {"number", T_INT, offsetof(Noddy, number), 0,
     "noddy number"},
```

```
    {NULL}  /* Sentinel */
};
```

We also need to update the `tp_init` handler to only allow strings [3] to be passed:

```
static int
Noddy_init(Noddy *self, PyObject *args, PyObject *kwds)
{
    PyObject *first=NULL, *last=NULL, *tmp;

    static char *kwlist[] = {"first", "last", "number", NULL};

    if (! PyArg_ParseTupleAndKeywords(args, kwds, "|SSi", kwlist,
                                      &first, &last,
                                      &self->number))
        return -1;

    if (first) {
        tmp = self->first;
        Py_INCREF(first);
        self->first = first;
        Py_DECREF(tmp);
    }

    if (last) {
        tmp = self->last;
        Py_INCREF(last);
        self->last = last;
        Py_DECREF(tmp);
    }

    return 0;
}
```

With these changes, we can assure that the `first` and `last` members are never *NULL* so we can remove checks for *NULL* values in almost all cases. This means that most of the `Py_XDECREF()` calls can be converted to `Py_DECREF()` calls. The only place we can't change these calls is in the deallocator, where there is the possibility that the initialization of these members failed in the constructor.

We also rename the module initialization function and module name in the initialization function, as we did before, and we add an extra definition to the `setup.py` file.

2.1.3 Supporting cyclic garbage collection

Python has a cyclic-garbage collector that can identify unneeded objects even when their reference counts are not zero. This can happen when objects are involved in cycles. For example, consider:

```
>>> l = []
>>> l.append(l)
>>> del l
```

In this example, we create a list that contains itself. When we delete it, it still has a reference from itself. Its reference count doesn't drop to zero. Fortunately, Python's cyclic-garbage collector will eventually figure out that the list is

---

[3] We now know that the first and last members are strings, so perhaps we could be less careful about decrementing their reference counts, however, we accept instances of string subclasses. Even though deallocating normal strings won't call back into our objects, we can't guarantee that deallocating an instance of a string subclass won't call back into our objects.

---

garbage and free it.

In the second version of the Noddy example, we allowed any kind of object to be stored in the first or last attributes. [4] This means that Noddy objects can participate in cycles:

```
>>> import noddy2
>>> n = noddy2.Noddy()
>>> l = [n]
>>> n.first = l
```

This is pretty silly, but it gives us an excuse to add support for the cyclic-garbage collector to the Noddy example. To support cyclic garbage collection, types need to fill two slots and set a class flag that enables these slots:

```c
#include <Python.h>
#include "structmember.h"

typedef struct {
    PyObject_HEAD
    PyObject *first;
    PyObject *last;
    int number;
} Noddy;

static int
Noddy_traverse(Noddy *self, visitproc visit, void *arg)
{
    int vret;

    if (self->first) {
        vret = visit(self->first, arg);
        if (vret != 0)
            return vret;
    }
    if (self->last) {
        vret = visit(self->last, arg);
        if (vret != 0)
            return vret;
    }

    return 0;
}

static int
Noddy_clear(Noddy *self)
{
    PyObject *tmp;

    tmp = self->first;
    self->first = NULL;
    Py_XDECREF(tmp);

    tmp = self->last;
    self->last = NULL;
    Py_XDECREF(tmp);
```

---

[4] Even in the third version, we aren't guaranteed to avoid cycles. Instances of string subclasses are allowed and string subclasses could allow cycles even if normal strings don't.

```
        return 0;
}

static void
Noddy_dealloc(Noddy* self)
{
    Noddy_clear(self);
    self->ob_type->tp_free((PyObject*)self);
}

static PyObject *
Noddy_new(PyTypeObject *type, PyObject *args, PyObject *kwds)
{
    Noddy *self;

    self = (Noddy *)type->tp_alloc(type, 0);
    if (self != NULL) {
        self->first = PyString_FromString("");
        if (self->first == NULL)
          {
            Py_DECREF(self);
            return NULL;
          }

        self->last = PyString_FromString("");
        if (self->last == NULL)
          {
            Py_DECREF(self);
            return NULL;
          }

        self->number = 0;
    }

    return (PyObject *)self;
}

static int
Noddy_init(Noddy *self, PyObject *args, PyObject *kwds)
{
    PyObject *first=NULL, *last=NULL, *tmp;

    static char *kwlist[] = {"first", "last", "number", NULL};

    if (! PyArg_ParseTupleAndKeywords(args, kwds, "|OOi", kwlist,
                                      &first, &last,
                                      &self->number))
        return -1;

    if (first) {
        tmp = self->first;
        Py_INCREF(first);
        self->first = first;
```

```
            Py_XDECREF(tmp);
        }

    if (last) {
        tmp = self->last;
        Py_INCREF(last);
        self->last = last;
        Py_XDECREF(tmp);
    }

    return 0;
}


static PyMemberDef Noddy_members[] = {
    {"first", T_OBJECT_EX, offsetof(Noddy, first), 0,
     "first name"},
    {"last", T_OBJECT_EX, offsetof(Noddy, last), 0,
     "last name"},
    {"number", T_INT, offsetof(Noddy, number), 0,
     "noddy number"},
    {NULL}  /* Sentinel */
};

static PyObject *
Noddy_name(Noddy* self)
{
    static PyObject *format = NULL;
    PyObject *args, *result;

    if (format == NULL) {
        format = PyString_FromString("%s %s");
        if (format == NULL)
            return NULL;
    }

    if (self->first == NULL) {
        PyErr_SetString(PyExc_AttributeError, "first");
        return NULL;
    }

    if (self->last == NULL) {
        PyErr_SetString(PyExc_AttributeError, "last");
        return NULL;
    }

    args = Py_BuildValue("OO", self->first, self->last);
    if (args == NULL)
        return NULL;

    result = PyString_Format(format, args);
    Py_DECREF(args);

    return result;
```

```
}

static PyMethodDef Noddy_methods[] = {
    {"name", (PyCFunction)Noddy_name, METH_NOARGS,
     "Return the name, combining the first and last name"
    },
    {NULL}  /* Sentinel */
};

static PyTypeObject NoddyType = {
    PyObject_HEAD_INIT(NULL)
    0,                         /*ob_size*/
    "noddy.Noddy",             /*tp_name*/
    sizeof(Noddy),             /*tp_basicsize*/
    0,                         /*tp_itemsize*/
    (destructor)Noddy_dealloc, /*tp_dealloc*/
    0,                         /*tp_print*/
    0,                         /*tp_getattr*/
    0,                         /*tp_setattr*/
    0,                         /*tp_compare*/
    0,                         /*tp_repr*/
    0,                         /*tp_as_number*/
    0,                         /*tp_as_sequence*/
    0,                         /*tp_as_mapping*/
    0,                         /*tp_hash */
    0,                         /*tp_call*/
    0,                         /*tp_str*/
    0,                         /*tp_getattro*/
    0,                         /*tp_setattro*/
    0,                         /*tp_as_buffer*/
    Py_TPFLAGS_DEFAULT | Py_TPFLAGS_BASETYPE | Py_TPFLAGS_HAVE_GC, /*tp_flags*/
    "Noddy objects",           /* tp_doc */
    (traverseproc)Noddy_traverse,   /* tp_traverse */
    (inquiry)Noddy_clear,           /* tp_clear */
    0,                              /* tp_richcompare */
    0,                              /* tp_weaklistoffset */
    0,                              /* tp_iter */
    0,                              /* tp_iternext */
    Noddy_methods,             /* tp_methods */
    Noddy_members,             /* tp_members */
    0,                         /* tp_getset */
    0,                         /* tp_base */
    0,                         /* tp_dict */
    0,                         /* tp_descr_get */
    0,                         /* tp_descr_set */
    0,                         /* tp_dictoffset */
    (initproc)Noddy_init,      /* tp_init */
    0,                         /* tp_alloc */
    Noddy_new,                 /* tp_new */
};

static PyMethodDef module_methods[] = {
    {NULL}  /* Sentinel */
};
```

```
#ifndef PyMODINIT_FUNC          /* declarations for DLL import/export */
#define PyMODINIT_FUNC void
#endif
PyMODINIT_FUNC
initnoddy4(void)
{
    PyObject* m;

    if (PyType_Ready(&NoddyType) < 0)
        return;

    m = Py_InitModule3("noddy4", module_methods,
                       "Example module that creates an extension type.");

    if (m == NULL)
      return;

    Py_INCREF(&NoddyType);
    PyModule_AddObject(m, "Noddy", (PyObject *)&NoddyType);
}
```

The traversal method provides access to subobjects that could participate in cycles:

```
static int
Noddy_traverse(Noddy *self, visitproc visit, void *arg)
{
    int vret;

    if (self->first) {
        vret = visit(self->first, arg);
        if (vret != 0)
            return vret;
    }
    if (self->last) {
        vret = visit(self->last, arg);
        if (vret != 0)
            return vret;
    }

    return 0;
}
```

For each subobject that can participate in cycles, we need to call the visit() function, which is passed to the traversal method. The visit() function takes as arguments the subobject and the extra argument *arg* passed to the traversal method. It returns an integer value that must be returned if it is non-zero.

Python 2.4 and higher provide a Py_VISIT() macro that automates calling visit functions. With Py_VISIT(), Noddy_traverse() can be simplified:

```
static int
Noddy_traverse(Noddy *self, visitproc visit, void *arg)
{
    Py_VISIT(self->first);
    Py_VISIT(self->last);
    return 0;
```

```
}
```

> **Note:** Note that the `tp_traverse` implementation must name its arguments exactly *visit* and *arg* in order to use `Py_VISIT()`. This is to encourage uniformity across these boring implementations.

We also need to provide a method for clearing any subobjects that can participate in cycles. We implement the method and reimplement the deallocator to use it:

```
static int
Noddy_clear(Noddy *self)
{
    PyObject *tmp;

    tmp = self->first;
    self->first = NULL;
    Py_XDECREF(tmp);

    tmp = self->last;
    self->last = NULL;
    Py_XDECREF(tmp);

    return 0;
}

static void
Noddy_dealloc(Noddy* self)
{
    Noddy_clear(self);
    self->ob_type->tp_free((PyObject*)self);
}
```

Notice the use of a temporary variable in `Noddy_clear()`. We use the temporary variable so that we can set each member to *NULL* before decrementing its reference count. We do this because, as was discussed earlier, if the reference count drops to zero, we might cause code to run that calls back into the object. In addition, because we now support garbage collection, we also have to worry about code being run that triggers garbage collection. If garbage collection is run, our `tp_traverse` handler could get called. We can't take a chance of having `Noddy_traverse()` called when a member's reference count has dropped to zero and its value hasn't been set to *NULL*.

Python 2.4 and higher provide a `Py_CLEAR()` that automates the careful decrementing of reference counts. With `Py_CLEAR()`, the `Noddy_clear()` function can be simplified:

```
static int
Noddy_clear(Noddy *self)
{
    Py_CLEAR(self->first);
    Py_CLEAR(self->last);
    return 0;
}
```

Finally, we add the `Py_TPFLAGS_HAVE_GC` flag to the class flags:

```
Py_TPFLAGS_DEFAULT | Py_TPFLAGS_BASETYPE | Py_TPFLAGS_HAVE_GC, /*tp_flags*/
```

That's pretty much it. If we had written custom `tp_alloc` or `tp_free` slots, we'd need to modify them for cyclic-garbage collection. Most extensions will use the versions automatically provided.

2.1.4 Subclassing other types

It is possible to create new extension types that are derived from existing types. It is easiest to inherit from the built in types, since an extension can easily use the PyTypeObject it needs. It can be difficult to share these PyTypeObject structures between extension modules.

In this example we will create a Shoddy type that inherits from the built-in list type. The new type will be completely compatible with regular lists, but will have an additional increment() method that increases an internal counter.

```
>>> import shoddy
>>> s = shoddy.Shoddy(range(3))
>>> s.extend(s)
>>> print len(s)
6
>>> print s.increment()
1
>>> print s.increment()
2

#include <Python.h>

typedef struct {
    PyListObject list;
    int state;
} Shoddy;


static PyObject *
Shoddy_increment(Shoddy *self, PyObject *unused)
{
    self->state++;
    return PyInt_FromLong(self->state);
}


static PyMethodDef Shoddy_methods[] = {
    {"increment", (PyCFunction)Shoddy_increment, METH_NOARGS,
     PyDoc_STR("increment state counter")},
    {NULL,          NULL},
};

static int
Shoddy_init(Shoddy *self, PyObject *args, PyObject *kwds)
{
    if (PyList_Type.tp_init((PyObject *)self, args, kwds) < 0)
        return -1;
    self->state = 0;
    return 0;
}


static PyTypeObject ShoddyType = {
    PyObject_HEAD_INIT(NULL)
    0,                          /* ob_size */
```

```
    "shoddy.Shoddy",              /* tp_name */
    sizeof(Shoddy),               /* tp_basicsize */
    0,                            /* tp_itemsize */
    0,                            /* tp_dealloc */
    0,                            /* tp_print */
    0,                            /* tp_getattr */
    0,                            /* tp_setattr */
    0,                            /* tp_compare */
    0,                            /* tp_repr */
    0,                            /* tp_as_number */
    0,                            /* tp_as_sequence */
    0,                            /* tp_as_mapping */
    0,                            /* tp_hash */
    0,                            /* tp_call */
    0,                            /* tp_str */
    0,                            /* tp_getattro */
    0,                            /* tp_setattro */
    0,                            /* tp_as_buffer */
    Py_TPFLAGS_DEFAULT |
      Py_TPFLAGS_BASETYPE,        /* tp_flags */
    0,                            /* tp_doc */
    0,                            /* tp_traverse */
    0,                            /* tp_clear */
    0,                            /* tp_richcompare */
    0,                            /* tp_weaklistoffset */
    0,                            /* tp_iter */
    0,                            /* tp_iternext */
    Shoddy_methods,               /* tp_methods */
    0,                            /* tp_members */
    0,                            /* tp_getset */
    0,                            /* tp_base */
    0,                            /* tp_dict */
    0,                            /* tp_descr_get */
    0,                            /* tp_descr_set */
    0,                            /* tp_dictoffset */
    (initproc)Shoddy_init,        /* tp_init */
    0,                            /* tp_alloc */
    0,                            /* tp_new */
};

PyMODINIT_FUNC
initshoddy(void)
{
    PyObject *m;

    ShoddyType.tp_base = &PyList_Type;
    if (PyType_Ready(&ShoddyType) < 0)
        return;

    m = Py_InitModule3("shoddy", NULL, "Shoddy module");
    if (m == NULL)
        return;

    Py_INCREF(&ShoddyType);
```

```
    PyModule_AddObject(m, "Shoddy", (PyObject *) &ShoddyType);
}
```

As you can see, the source code closely resembles the Noddy examples in previous sections. We will break down the main differences between them.

```
typedef struct {
    PyListObject list;
    int state;
} Shoddy;
```

The primary difference for derived type objects is that the base type's object structure must be the first value. The base type will already include the PyObject_HEAD() at the beginning of its structure.

When a Python object is a Shoddy instance, its *PyObject** pointer can be safely cast to both *PyListObject** and *Shoddy**.

```
static int
Shoddy_init(Shoddy *self, PyObject *args, PyObject *kwds)
{
    if (PyList_Type.tp_init((PyObject *)self, args, kwds) < 0)
        return -1;
    self->state = 0;
    return 0;
}
```

In the __init__ method for our type, we can see how to call through to the __init__ method of the base type.

This pattern is important when writing a type with custom new and dealloc methods. The new method should not actually create the memory for the object with tp_alloc, that will be handled by the base class when calling its tp_new.

When filling out the PyTypeObject() for the Shoddy type, you see a slot for tp_base(). Due to cross platform compiler issues, you can't fill that field directly with the PyList_Type(); it can be done later in the module's init() function.

```
PyMODINIT_FUNC
initshoddy(void)
{
    PyObject *m;

    ShoddyType.tp_base = &PyList_Type;
    if (PyType_Ready(&ShoddyType) < 0)
        return;

    m = Py_InitModule3("shoddy", NULL, "Shoddy module");
    if (m == NULL)
        return;

    Py_INCREF(&ShoddyType);
    PyModule_AddObject(m, "Shoddy", (PyObject *) &ShoddyType);
}
```

Before calling PyType_Ready(), the type structure must have the tp_base slot filled in. When we are deriving a new type, it is not necessary to fill out the tp_alloc slot with PyType_GenericNew() – the allocate function from the base type will be inherited.

After that, calling PyType_Ready() and adding the type object to the module is the same as with the basic Noddy examples.

2.2 Type Methods

This section aims to give a quick fly-by on the various type methods you can implement and what they do.

Here is the definition of `PyTypeObject`, with some fields only used in debug builds omitted:

```
typedef struct _typeobject {
    PyObject_VAR_HEAD
    char *tp_name; /* For printing, in format "<module>.<name>" */
    int tp_basicsize, tp_itemsize; /* For allocation */

    /* Methods to implement standard operations */

    destructor tp_dealloc;
    printfunc tp_print;
    getattrfunc tp_getattr;
    setattrfunc tp_setattr;
    cmpfunc tp_compare;
    reprfunc tp_repr;

    /* Method suites for standard classes */

    PyNumberMethods *tp_as_number;
    PySequenceMethods *tp_as_sequence;
    PyMappingMethods *tp_as_mapping;

    /* More standard operations (here for binary compatibility) */

    hashfunc tp_hash;
    ternaryfunc tp_call;
    reprfunc tp_str;
    getattrofunc tp_getattro;
    setattrofunc tp_setattro;

    /* Functions to access object as input/output buffer */
    PyBufferProcs *tp_as_buffer;

    /* Flags to define presence of optional/expanded features */
    long tp_flags;

    char *tp_doc; /* Documentation string */

    /* Assigned meaning in release 2.0 */
    /* call function for all accessible objects */
    traverseproc tp_traverse;

    /* delete references to contained objects */
    inquiry tp_clear;

    /* Assigned meaning in release 2.1 */
    /* rich comparisons */
    richcmpfunc tp_richcompare;

    /* weak reference enabler */
```

```
    long tp_weaklistoffset;

    /* Added in release 2.2 */
    /* Iterators */
    getiterfunc tp_iter;
    iternextfunc tp_iternext;

    /* Attribute descriptor and subclassing stuff */
    struct PyMethodDef *tp_methods;
    struct PyMemberDef *tp_members;
    struct PyGetSetDef *tp_getset;
    struct _typeobject *tp_base;
    PyObject *tp_dict;
    descrgetfunc tp_descr_get;
    descrsetfunc tp_descr_set;
    long tp_dictoffset;
    initproc tp_init;
    allocfunc tp_alloc;
    newfunc tp_new;
    freefunc tp_free; /* Low-level free-memory routine */
    inquiry tp_is_gc; /* For PyObject_IS_GC */
    PyObject *tp_bases;
    PyObject *tp_mro; /* method resolution order */
    PyObject *tp_cache;
    PyObject *tp_subclasses;
    PyObject *tp_weaklist;

} PyTypeObject;
```

Now that's a *lot* of methods. Don't worry too much though - if you have a type you want to define, the chances are very good that you will only implement a handful of these.

As you probably expect by now, we're going to go over this and give more information about the various handlers. We won't go in the order they are defined in the structure, because there is a lot of historical baggage that impacts the ordering of the fields; be sure your type initialization keeps the fields in the right order! It's often easiest to find an example that includes all the fields you need (even if they're initialized to 0) and then change the values to suit your new type.

```
char *tp_name; /* For printing */
```

The name of the type - as mentioned in the last section, this will appear in various places, almost entirely for diagnostic purposes. Try to choose something that will be helpful in such a situation!

```
int tp_basicsize, tp_itemsize; /* For allocation */
```

These fields tell the runtime how much memory to allocate when new objects of this type are created. Python has some built-in support for variable length structures (think: strings, lists) which is where the `tp_itemsize` field comes in. This will be dealt with later.

```
char *tp_doc;
```

Here you can put a string (or its address) that you want returned when the Python script references `obj.__doc__` to retrieve the doc string.

Now we come to the basic type methods—the ones most extension types will implement.

2.2.1 Finalization and De-allocation

```
destructor tp_dealloc;
```

This function is called when the reference count of the instance of your type is reduced to zero and the Python interpreter wants to reclaim it. If your type has memory to free or other clean-up to perform, put it here. The object itself needs to be freed here as well. Here is an example of this function:

```
static void
newdatatype_dealloc(newdatatypeobject * obj)
{
    free(obj->obj_UnderlyingDatatypePtr);
    obj->ob_type->tp_free(obj);
}
```

One important requirement of the deallocator function is that it leaves any pending exceptions alone. This is important since deallocators are frequently called as the interpreter unwinds the Python stack; when the stack is unwound due to an exception (rather than normal returns), nothing is done to protect the deallocators from seeing that an exception has already been set. Any actions which a deallocator performs which may cause additional Python code to be executed may detect that an exception has been set. This can lead to misleading errors from the interpreter. The proper way to protect against this is to save a pending exception before performing the unsafe action, and restoring it when done. This can be done using the PyErr_Fetch() and PyErr_Restore() functions:

```
static void
my_dealloc(PyObject *obj)
{
    MyObject *self = (MyObject *) obj;
    PyObject *cbresult;

    if (self->my_callback != NULL) {
        PyObject *err_type, *err_value, *err_traceback;
        int have_error = PyErr_Occurred() ? 1 : 0;

        if (have_error)
            PyErr_Fetch(&err_type, &err_value, &err_traceback);

        cbresult = PyObject_CallObject(self->my_callback, NULL);
        if (cbresult == NULL)
            PyErr_WriteUnraisable(self->my_callback);
        else
            Py_DECREF(cbresult);

        if (have_error)
            PyErr_Restore(err_type, err_value, err_traceback);

        Py_DECREF(self->my_callback);
    }
    obj->ob_type->tp_free((PyObject*)self);
}
```

2.2.2 Object Presentation

In Python, there are three ways to generate a textual representation of an object: the repr() function (or equivalent back-tick syntax), the str() function, and the print statement. For most objects, the print statement is equivalent to the str() function, but it is possible to special-case printing to a FILE* if necessary; this should only be done if efficiency is identified as a problem and profiling suggests that creating a temporary string object to be written to a file is too expensive.

These handlers are all optional, and most types at most need to implement the `tp_str` and `tp_repr` handlers.

```
reprfunc tp_repr;
reprfunc tp_str;
printfunc tp_print;
```

The `tp_repr` handler should return a string object containing a representation of the instance for which it is called. Here is a simple example:

```
static PyObject *
newdatatype_repr(newdatatypeobject * obj)
{
    return PyString_FromFormat("Repr-ified_newdatatype{{size:\%d}}",
                               obj->obj_UnderlyingDatatypePtr->size);
}
```

If no `tp_repr` handler is specified, the interpreter will supply a representation that uses the type's `tp_name` and a uniquely-identifying value for the object.

The `tp_str` handler is to `str()` what the `tp_repr` handler described above is to `repr()`; that is, it is called when Python code calls `str()` on an instance of your object. Its implementation is very similar to the `tp_repr` function, but the resulting string is intended for human consumption. If `tp_str` is not specified, the `tp_repr` handler is used instead.

Here is a simple example:

```
static PyObject *
newdatatype_str(newdatatypeobject * obj)
{
    return PyString_FromFormat("Stringified_newdatatype{{size:\%d}}",
                               obj->obj_UnderlyingDatatypePtr->size);
}
```

The print function will be called whenever Python needs to "print" an instance of the type. For example, if 'node' is an instance of type TreeNode, then the print function is called when Python code calls:

```
print node
```

There is a flags argument and one flag, `Py_PRINT_RAW`, and it suggests that you print without string quotes and possibly without interpreting escape sequences.

The print function receives a file object as an argument. You will likely want to write to that file object.

Here is a sample print function:

```
static int
newdatatype_print(newdatatypeobject *obj, FILE *fp, int flags)
{
    if (flags & Py_PRINT_RAW) {
        fprintf(fp, "<{newdatatype object--size: %d}>",
                obj->obj_UnderlyingDatatypePtr->size);
    }
    else {
        fprintf(fp, "\"<{newdatatype object--size: %d}>\"",
                obj->obj_UnderlyingDatatypePtr->size);
    }
    return 0;
}
```

2.2.3 Attribute Management

For every object which can support attributes, the corresponding type must provide the functions that control how the attributes are resolved. There needs to be a function which can retrieve attributes (if any are defined), and another to set attributes (if setting attributes is allowed). Removing an attribute is a special case, for which the new value passed to the handler is *NULL*.

Python supports two pairs of attribute handlers; a type that supports attributes only needs to implement the functions for one pair. The difference is that one pair takes the name of the attribute as a `char*`, while the other accepts a `PyObject*`. Each type can use whichever pair makes more sense for the implementation's convenience.

```
getattrfunc   tp_getattr;        /* char * version */
setattrfunc   tp_setattr;
/* ... */
getattrofunc  tp_getattrofunc;   /* PyObject * version */
setattrofunc  tp_setattrofunc;
```

If accessing attributes of an object is always a simple operation (this will be explained shortly), there are generic implementations which can be used to provide the `PyObject*` version of the attribute management functions. The actual need for type-specific attribute handlers almost completely disappeared starting with Python 2.2, though there are many examples which have not been updated to use some of the new generic mechanism that is available.

Generic Attribute Management

New in version 2.2.

Most extension types only use *simple* attributes. So, what makes the attributes simple? There are only a couple of conditions that must be met:

1. The name of the attributes must be known when `PyType_Ready()` is called.

2. No special processing is needed to record that an attribute was looked up or set, nor do actions need to be taken based on the value.

Note that this list does not place any restrictions on the values of the attributes, when the values are computed, or how relevant data is stored.

When `PyType_Ready()` is called, it uses three tables referenced by the type object to create *descriptor*s which are placed in the dictionary of the type object. Each descriptor controls access to one attribute of the instance object. Each of the tables is optional; if all three are *NULL*, instances of the type will only have attributes that are inherited from their base type, and should leave the `tp_getattro` and `tp_setattro` fields *NULL* as well, allowing the base type to handle attributes.

The tables are declared as three fields of the type object:

```
struct PyMethodDef *tp_methods;
struct PyMemberDef *tp_members;
struct PyGetSetDef *tp_getset;
```

If `tp_methods` is not *NULL*, it must refer to an array of `PyMethodDef` structures. Each entry in the table is an instance of this structure:

```
typedef struct PyMethodDef {
    char        *ml_name;    /* method name */
    PyCFunction ml_meth;     /* implementation function */
    int         ml_flags;    /* flags */
    char        *ml_doc;     /* docstring */
} PyMethodDef;
```

One entry should be defined for each method provided by the type; no entries are needed for methods inherited from a base type. One additional entry is needed at the end; it is a sentinel that marks the end of the array. The `ml_name` field of the sentinel must be *NULL*.

XXX Need to refer to some unified discussion of the structure fields, shared with the next section.

The second table is used to define attributes which map directly to data stored in the instance. A variety of primitive C types are supported, and access may be read-only or read-write. The structures in the table are defined as:

```
typedef struct PyMemberDef {
    char *name;
    int  type;
    int  offset;
    int  flags;
    char *doc;
} PyMemberDef;
```

For each entry in the table, a *descriptor* will be constructed and added to the type which will be able to extract a value from the instance structure. The `type` field should contain one of the type codes defined in the `structmember.h` header; the value will be used to determine how to convert Python values to and from C values. The `flags` field is used to store flags which control how the attribute can be accessed.

XXX Need to move some of this to a shared section!

The following flag constants are defined in `structmember.h`; they may be combined using bitwise-OR.

Constant	Meaning
READONLY	Never writable.
RO	Shorthand for READONLY.
READ_RESTRICTED	Not readable in restricted mode.
WRITE_RESTRICTED	Not writable in restricted mode.
RESTRICTED	Not readable or writable in restricted mode.

An interesting advantage of using the `tp_members` table to build descriptors that are used at runtime is that any attribute defined this way can have an associated doc string simply by providing the text in the table. An application can use the introspection API to retrieve the descriptor from the class object, and get the doc string using its `__doc__` attribute.

As with the `tp_methods` table, a sentinel entry with a `name` value of *NULL* is required.

Type-specific Attribute Management

For simplicity, only the `char*` version will be demonstrated here; the type of the name parameter is the only difference between the `char*` and `PyObject*` flavors of the interface. This example effectively does the same thing as the generic example above, but does not use the generic support added in Python 2.2. The value in showing this is two-fold: it demonstrates how basic attribute management can be done in a way that is portable to older versions of Python, and explains how the handler functions are called, so that if you do need to extend their functionality, you'll understand what needs to be done.

The `tp_getattr` handler is called when the object requires an attribute look-up. It is called in the same situations where the `__getattr__()` method of a class would be called.

A likely way to handle this is (1) to implement a set of functions (such as `newdatatype_getSize()` and `newdatatype_setSize()` in the example below), (2) provide a method table listing these functions, and (3) provide a getattr function that returns the result of a lookup in that table. The method table uses the same structure as the `tp_methods` field of the type object.

Here is an example:

```
static PyMethodDef newdatatype_methods[] = {
    {"getSize", (PyCFunction)newdatatype_getSize, METH_VARARGS,
     "Return the current size."},
    {"setSize", (PyCFunction)newdatatype_setSize, METH_VARARGS,
     "Set the size."},
    {NULL, NULL, 0, NULL}            /* sentinel */
};

static PyObject *
newdatatype_getattr(newdatatypeobject *obj, char *name)
{
    return Py_FindMethod(newdatatype_methods, (PyObject *)obj, name);
}
```

The tp_setattr handler is called when the __setattr__() or __delattr__() method of a class instance would be called. When an attribute should be deleted, the third parameter will be *NULL*. Here is an example that simply raises an exception; if this were really all you wanted, the tp_setattr handler should be set to *NULL*.

```
static int
newdatatype_setattr(newdatatypeobject *obj, char *name, PyObject *v)
{
    (void)PyErr_Format(PyExc_RuntimeError, "Read-only attribute: \%s", name);
    return -1;
}
```

2.2.4 Object Comparison

```
cmpfunc tp_compare;
```

The tp_compare handler is called when comparisons are needed and the object does not implement the specific rich comparison method which matches the requested comparison. (It is always used if defined and the PyObject_Compare() or PyObject_Cmp() functions are used, or if cmp() is used from Python.) It is analogous to the __cmp__() method. This function should return −1 if *obj1* is less than *obj2*, 0 if they are equal, and 1 if *obj1* is greater than *obj2*. (It was previously allowed to return arbitrary negative or positive integers for less than and greater than, respectively; as of Python 2.2, this is no longer allowed. In the future, other return values may be assigned a different meaning.)

A tp_compare handler may raise an exception. In this case it should return a negative value. The caller has to test for the exception using PyErr_Occurred().

Here is a sample implementation:

```
static int
newdatatype_compare(newdatatypeobject * obj1, newdatatypeobject * obj2)
{
    long result;

    if (obj1->obj_UnderlyingDatatypePtr->size <
        obj2->obj_UnderlyingDatatypePtr->size) {
        result = -1;
    }
    else if (obj1->obj_UnderlyingDatatypePtr->size >
            obj2->obj_UnderlyingDatatypePtr->size) {
        result = 1;
    }
    else {
```

```
        result = 0;
    }
    return result;
}
```

2.2.5 Abstract Protocol Support

Python supports a variety of *abstract* 'protocols;' the specific interfaces provided to use these interfaces are documented in *abstract*.

A number of these abstract interfaces were defined early in the development of the Python implementation. In particular, the number, mapping, and sequence protocols have been part of Python since the beginning. Other protocols have been added over time. For protocols which depend on several handler routines from the type implementation, the older protocols have been defined as optional blocks of handlers referenced by the type object. For newer protocols there are additional slots in the main type object, with a flag bit being set to indicate that the slots are present and should be checked by the interpreter. (The flag bit does not indicate that the slot values are non-*NULL*. The flag may be set to indicate the presence of a slot, but a slot may still be unfilled.)

```
PyNumberMethods    *tp_as_number;
PySequenceMethods  *tp_as_sequence;
PyMappingMethods   *tp_as_mapping;
```

If you wish your object to be able to act like a number, a sequence, or a mapping object, then you place the address of a structure that implements the C type `PyNumberMethods`, `PySequenceMethods`, or `PyMappingMethods`, respectively. It is up to you to fill in this structure with appropriate values. You can find examples of the use of each of these in the `Objects` directory of the Python source distribution.

```
hashfunc tp_hash;
```

This function, if you choose to provide it, should return a hash number for an instance of your data type. Here is a moderately pointless example:

```
static long
newdatatype_hash(newdatatypeobject *obj)
{
    long result;
    result = obj->obj_UnderlyingDatatypePtr->size;
    result = result * 3;
    return result;
}
```

```
ternaryfunc tp_call;
```

This function is called when an instance of your data type is "called", for example, if `obj1` is an instance of your data type and the Python script contains `obj1('hello')`, the `tp_call` handler is invoked.

This function takes three arguments:

1. *arg1* is the instance of the data type which is the subject of the call. If the call is `obj1('hello')`, then *arg1* is `obj1`.

2. *arg2* is a tuple containing the arguments to the call. You can use `PyArg_ParseTuple()` to extract the arguments.

3. *arg3* is a dictionary of keyword arguments that were passed. If this is non-*NULL* and you support keyword arguments, use `PyArg_ParseTupleAndKeywords()` to extract the arguments. If you do not want to support keyword arguments and this is non-*NULL*, raise a `TypeError` with a message saying that keyword arguments are not supported.

Here is a desultory example of the implementation of the call function.

```
/* Implement the call function.
 *    obj1 is the instance receiving the call.
 *    obj2 is a tuple containing the arguments to the call, in this
 *        case 3 strings.
 */
static PyObject *
newdatatype_call(newdatatypeobject *obj, PyObject *args, PyObject *other)
{
    PyObject *result;
    char *arg1;
    char *arg2;
    char *arg3;

    if (!PyArg_ParseTuple(args, "sss:call", &arg1, &arg2, &arg3)) {
        return NULL;
    }
    result = PyString_FromFormat(
        "Returning -- value: [\%d] arg1: [\%s] arg2: [\%s] arg3: [\%s]\n",
        obj->obj_UnderlyingDatatypePtr->size,
        arg1, arg2, arg3);
    printf("\%s", PyString_AS_STRING(result));
    return result;
}
```

XXX some fields need to be added here...

```
/* Added in release 2.2 */
/* Iterators */
getiterfunc tp_iter;
iternextfunc tp_iternext;
```

These functions provide support for the iterator protocol. Any object which wishes to support iteration over its contents (which may be generated during iteration) must implement the `tp_iter` handler. Objects which are returned by a `tp_iter` handler must implement both the `tp_iter` and `tp_iternext` handlers. Both handlers take exactly one parameter, the instance for which they are being called, and return a new reference. In the case of an error, they should set an exception and return *NULL*.

For an object which represents an iterable collection, the `tp_iter` handler must return an iterator object. The iterator object is responsible for maintaining the state of the iteration. For collections which can support multiple iterators which do not interfere with each other (as lists and tuples do), a new iterator should be created and returned. Objects which can only be iterated over once (usually due to side effects of iteration) should implement this handler by returning a new reference to themselves, and should also implement the `tp_iternext` handler. File objects are an example of such an iterator.

Iterator objects should implement both handlers. The `tp_iter` handler should return a new reference to the iterator (this is the same as the `tp_iter` handler for objects which can only be iterated over destructively). The `tp_iternext` handler should return a new reference to the next object in the iteration if there is one. If the iteration has reached the end, it may return *NULL* without setting an exception or it may set `StopIteration`; avoiding the exception can yield slightly better performance. If an actual error occurs, it should set an exception and return *NULL*.

2.2.6 Weak Reference Support

One of the goals of Python's weak-reference implementation is to allow any type to participate in the weak reference mechanism without incurring the overhead on those objects which do not benefit by weak referencing (such as numbers).

For an object to be weakly referencable, the extension must include a `PyObject *` field in the instance structure for the use of the weak reference mechanism; it must be initialized to *NULL* by the object's constructor. It must also set the `tp_weaklistoffset` field of the corresponding type object to the offset of the field. For example, the instance type is defined with the following structure:

```
typedef struct {
    PyObject_HEAD
    PyClassObject *in_class;       /* The class object */
    PyObject      *in_dict;        /* A dictionary */
    PyObject      *in_weakreflist; /* List of weak references */
} PyInstanceObject;
```

The statically-declared type object for instances is defined this way:

```
PyTypeObject PyInstance_Type = {
    PyObject_HEAD_INIT(&PyType_Type)
    0,
    "module.instance",

    /* Lots of stuff omitted for brevity... */

    Py_TPFLAGS_DEFAULT,                           /* tp_flags */
    0,                                            /* tp_doc */
    0,                                            /* tp_traverse */
    0,                                            /* tp_clear */
    0,                                            /* tp_richcompare */
    offsetof(PyInstanceObject, in_weakreflist),   /* tp_weaklistoffset */
};
```

The type constructor is responsible for initializing the weak reference list to *NULL*:

```
static PyObject *
instance_new() {
    /* Other initialization stuff omitted for brevity */

    self->in_weakreflist = NULL;

    return (PyObject *) self;
}
```

The only further addition is that the destructor needs to call the weak reference manager to clear any weak references. This is only required if the weak reference list is non-*NULL*:

```
static void
instance_dealloc(PyInstanceObject *inst)
{
    /* Allocate temporaries if needed, but do not begin
       destruction just yet.
     */

    if (inst->in_weakreflist != NULL)
        PyObject_ClearWeakRefs((PyObject *) inst);

    /* Proceed with object destruction normally. */
}
```

2.2.7 More Suggestions

Remember that you can omit most of these functions, in which case you provide 0 as a value. There are type definitions for each of the functions you must provide. They are in `object.h` in the Python include directory that comes with the source distribution of Python.

In order to learn how to implement any specific method for your new data type, do the following: Download and unpack the Python source distribution. Go the `Objects` directory, then search the C source files for `tp_` plus the function you want (for example, `tp_print` or `tp_compare`). You will find examples of the function you want to implement.

When you need to verify that an object is an instance of the type you are implementing, use the `PyObject_TypeCheck()` function. A sample of its use might be something like the following:

```
if (! PyObject_TypeCheck(some_object, &MyType)) {
    PyErr_SetString(PyExc_TypeError, "arg #1 not a mything");
    return NULL;
}
```

BUILDING C AND C++ EXTENSIONS WITH DISTUTILS

Starting in Python 1.4, Python provides, on Unix, a special make file for building make files for building dynamically-linked extensions and custom interpreters. Starting with Python 2.0, this mechanism (known as related to Makefile.pre.in, and Setup files) is no longer supported. Building custom interpreters was rarely used, and extension modules can be built using distutils.

Building an extension module using distutils requires that distutils is installed on the build machine, which is included in Python 2.x and available separately for Python 1.5. Since distutils also supports creation of binary packages, users don't necessarily need a compiler and distutils to install the extension.

A distutils package contains a driver script, `setup.py`. This is a plain Python file, which, in the most simple case, could look like this:

```
from distutils.core import setup, Extension

module1 = Extension('demo',
                    sources = ['demo.c'])

setup (name = 'PackageName',
       version = '1.0',
       description = 'This is a demo package',
       ext_modules = [module1])
```

With this `setup.py`, and a file `demo.c`, running

```
python setup.py build
```

will compile `demo.c`, and produce an extension module named `demo` in the `build` directory. Depending on the system, the module file will end up in a subdirectory `build/lib.system`, and may have a name like `demo.so` or `demo.pyd`.

In the `setup.py`, all execution is performed by calling the `setup` function. This takes a variable number of keyword arguments, of which the example above uses only a subset. Specifically, the example specifies meta-information to build packages, and it specifies the contents of the package. Normally, a package will contain of addition modules, like Python source modules, documentation, subpackages, etc. Please refer to the distutils documentation in *distutils-index* to learn more about the features of distutils; this section explains building extension modules only.

It is common to pre-compute arguments to `setup()`, to better structure the driver script. In the example above, the `ext_modules` argument to `setup()` is a list of extension modules, each of which is an instance of the `Extension`. In the example, the instance defines an extension named `demo` which is build by compiling a single source file, `demo.c`.

In many cases, building an extension is more complex, since additional preprocessor defines and libraries may be needed. This is demonstrated in the example below.

```
from distutils.core import setup, Extension
```

```
module1 = Extension('demo',
                    define_macros = [('MAJOR_VERSION', '1'),
                                     ('MINOR_VERSION', '0')],
                    include_dirs = ['/usr/local/include'],
                    libraries = ['tcl83'],
                    library_dirs = ['/usr/local/lib'],
                    sources = ['demo.c'])

setup (name = 'PackageName',
       version = '1.0',
       description = 'This is a demo package',
       author = 'Martin v. Loewis',
       author_email = 'martin@v.loewis.de',
       url = 'https://docs.python.org/extending/building',
       long_description = '''
This is really just a demo package.
''',
       ext_modules = [module1])
```

In this example, `setup()` is called with additional meta-information, which is recommended when distribution packages have to be built. For the extension itself, it specifies preprocessor defines, include directories, library directories, and libraries. Depending on the compiler, distutils passes this information in different ways to the compiler. For example, on Unix, this may result in the compilation commands

```
gcc -DNDEBUG -g -O3 -Wall -Wstrict-prototypes -fPIC -DMAJOR_VERSION=1 -DMINOR_VERSION=
```

```
gcc -shared build/temp.linux-i686-2.2/demo.o -L/usr/local/lib -ltcl83 -o build/lib.lin
```

These lines are for demonstration purposes only; distutils users should trust that distutils gets the invocations right.

3.1 Distributing your extension modules

When an extension has been successfully build, there are three ways to use it.

End-users will typically want to install the module, they do so by running

```
python setup.py install
```

Module maintainers should produce source packages; to do so, they run

```
python setup.py sdist
```

In some cases, additional files need to be included in a source distribution; this is done through a `MANIFEST.in` file; see the distutils documentation for details.

If the source distribution has been build successfully, maintainers can also create binary distributions. Depending on the platform, one of the following commands can be used to do so.

```
python setup.py bdist_wininst
python setup.py bdist_rpm
python setup.py bdist_dumb
```

BUILDING C AND C++ EXTENSIONS ON WINDOWS

This chapter briefly explains how to create a Windows extension module for Python using Microsoft Visual C++, and follows with more detailed background information on how it works. The explanatory material is useful for both the Windows programmer learning to build Python extensions and the Unix programmer interested in producing software which can be successfully built on both Unix and Windows.

Module authors are encouraged to use the distutils approach for building extension modules, instead of the one described in this section. You will still need the C compiler that was used to build Python; typically Microsoft Visual C++.

Note: This chapter mentions a number of filenames that include an encoded Python version number. These filenames are represented with the version number shown as XY; in practice, ′X′ will be the major version number and ′Y′ will be the minor version number of the Python release you're working with. For example, if you are using Python 2.2.1, XY will actually be 22.

4.1 A Cookbook Approach

There are two approaches to building extension modules on Windows, just as there are on Unix: use the distutils package to control the build process, or do things manually. The distutils approach works well for most extensions; documentation on using distutils to build and package extension modules is available in *distutils-index*. If you find you really need to do things manually, it may be instructive to study the project file for the winsound standard library module.

4.2 Differences Between Unix and Windows

Unix and Windows use completely different paradigms for run-time loading of code. Before you try to build a module that can be dynamically loaded, be aware of how your system works.

In Unix, a shared object (.so) file contains code to be used by the program, and also the names of functions and data that it expects to find in the program. When the file is joined to the program, all references to those functions and data in the file's code are changed to point to the actual locations in the program where the functions and data are placed in memory. This is basically a link operation.

In Windows, a dynamic-link library (.dll) file has no dangling references. Instead, an access to functions or data goes through a lookup table. So the DLL code does not have to be fixed up at runtime to refer to the program's memory; instead, the code already uses the DLL's lookup table, and the lookup table is modified at runtime to point to the functions and data.

In Unix, there is only one type of library file (.a) which contains code from several object files (.o). During the link step to create a shared object file (.so), the linker may find that it doesn't know where an identifier is defined. The linker will look for it in the object files in the libraries; if it finds it, it will include all the code from that object file.

In Windows, there are two types of library, a static library and an import library (both called .lib). A static library is like a Unix .a file; it contains code to be included as necessary. An import library is basically used only to reassure the linker that a certain identifier is legal, and will be present in the program when the DLL is loaded. So the linker uses the information from the import library to build the lookup table for using identifiers that are not included in the DLL. When an application or a DLL is linked, an import library may be generated, which will need to be used for all future DLLs that depend on the symbols in the application or DLL.

Suppose you are building two dynamic-load modules, B and C, which should share another block of code A. On Unix, you would *not* pass A.a to the linker for B.so and C.so; that would cause it to be included twice, so that B and C would each have their own copy. In Windows, building A.dll will also build A.lib. You *do* pass A.lib to the linker for B and C. A.lib does not contain code; it just contains information which will be used at runtime to access A's code.

In Windows, using an import library is sort of like using import spam; it gives you access to spam's names, but does not create a separate copy. On Unix, linking with a library is more like from spam import *; it does create a separate copy.

4.3 Using DLLs in Practice

Windows Python is built in Microsoft Visual C++; using other compilers may or may not work (though Borland seems to). The rest of this section is MSVC++ specific.

When creating DLLs in Windows, you must pass pythonXY.lib to the linker. To build two DLLs, spam and ni (which uses C functions found in spam), you could use these commands:

```
cl /LD /I/python/include spam.c ../libs/pythonXY.lib
cl /LD /I/python/include ni.c spam.lib ../libs/pythonXY.lib
```

The first command created three files: spam.obj, spam.dll and spam.lib. Spam.dll does not contain any Python functions (such as PyArg_ParseTuple()), but it does know how to find the Python code thanks to pythonXY.lib.

The second command created ni.dll (and .obj and .lib), which knows how to find the necessary functions from spam, and also from the Python executable.

Not every identifier is exported to the lookup table. If you want any other modules (including Python) to be able to see your identifiers, you have to say _declspec(dllexport), as in void _declspec(dllexport) initspam(void) or PyObject _declspec(dllexport) *NiGetSpamData(void).

Developer Studio will throw in a lot of import libraries that you do not really need, adding about 100K to your executable. To get rid of them, use the Project Settings dialog, Link tab, to specify *ignore default libraries*. Add the correct msvcrtxx.lib to the list of libraries.

EMBEDDING PYTHON IN ANOTHER APPLICATION

The previous chapters discussed how to extend Python, that is, how to extend the functionality of Python by attaching a library of C functions to it. It is also possible to do it the other way around: enrich your C/C++ application by embedding Python in it. Embedding provides your application with the ability to implement some of the functionality of your application in Python rather than C or C++. This can be used for many purposes; one example would be to allow users to tailor the application to their needs by writing some scripts in Python. You can also use it yourself if some of the functionality can be written in Python more easily.

Embedding Python is similar to extending it, but not quite. The difference is that when you extend Python, the main program of the application is still the Python interpreter, while if you embed Python, the main program may have nothing to do with Python — instead, some parts of the application occasionally call the Python interpreter to run some Python code.

So if you are embedding Python, you are providing your own main program. One of the things this main program has to do is initialize the Python interpreter. At the very least, you have to call the function `Py_Initialize()`. There are optional calls to pass command line arguments to Python. Then later you can call the interpreter from any part of the application.

There are several different ways to call the interpreter: you can pass a string containing Python statements to `PyRun_SimpleString()`, or you can pass a stdio file pointer and a file name (for identification in error messages only) to `PyRun_SimpleFile()`. You can also call the lower-level operations described in the previous chapters to construct and use Python objects.

A simple demo of embedding Python can be found in the directory `Demo/embed/` of the source distribution.

See also:

c-api-index The details of Python's C interface are given in this manual. A great deal of necessary information can be found here.

5.1 Very High Level Embedding

The simplest form of embedding Python is the use of the very high level interface. This interface is intended to execute a Python script without needing to interact with the application directly. This can for example be used to perform some operation on a file.

```
#include <Python.h>

int
main(int argc, char *argv[])
{
    Py_SetProgramName(argv[0]);  /* optional but recommended */
    Py_Initialize();
    PyRun_SimpleString("from time import time,ctime\n"
```

```
                          "print 'Today is',ctime(time())\n");
    Py_Finalize();
    return 0;
}
```

The `Py_SetProgramName()` function should be called before `Py_Initialize()` to inform the interpreter about paths to Python run-time libraries. Next, the Python interpreter is initialized with `Py_Initialize()`, followed by the execution of a hard-coded Python script that prints the date and time. Afterwards, the `Py_Finalize()` call shuts the interpreter down, followed by the end of the program. In a real program, you may want to get the Python script from another source, perhaps a text-editor routine, a file, or a database. Getting the Python code from a file can better be done by using the `PyRun_SimpleFile()` function, which saves you the trouble of allocating memory space and loading the file contents.

5.2 Beyond Very High Level Embedding: An overview

The high level interface gives you the ability to execute arbitrary pieces of Python code from your application, but exchanging data values is quite cumbersome to say the least. If you want that, you should use lower level calls. At the cost of having to write more C code, you can achieve almost anything.

It should be noted that extending Python and embedding Python is quite the same activity, despite the different intent. Most topics discussed in the previous chapters are still valid. To show this, consider what the extension code from Python to C really does:

1. Convert data values from Python to C,

2. Perform a function call to a C routine using the converted values, and

3. Convert the data values from the call from C to Python.

When embedding Python, the interface code does:

1. Convert data values from C to Python,

2. Perform a function call to a Python interface routine using the converted values, and

3. Convert the data values from the call from Python to C.

As you can see, the data conversion steps are simply swapped to accommodate the different direction of the cross-language transfer. The only difference is the routine that you call between both data conversions. When extending, you call a C routine, when embedding, you call a Python routine.

This chapter will not discuss how to convert data from Python to C and vice versa. Also, proper use of references and dealing with errors is assumed to be understood. Since these aspects do not differ from extending the interpreter, you can refer to earlier chapters for the required information.

5.3 Pure Embedding

The first program aims to execute a function in a Python script. Like in the section about the very high level interface, the Python interpreter does not directly interact with the application (but that will change in the next section).

The code to run a function defined in a Python script is:

```
#include <Python.h>

int
main(int argc, char *argv[])
{
```

```
PyObject *pName, *pModule, *pDict, *pFunc;
PyObject *pArgs, *pValue;
int i;

if (argc < 3) {
    fprintf(stderr,"Usage: call pythonfile funcname [args]\n");
    return 1;
}

Py_Initialize();
pName = PyString_FromString(argv[1]);
/* Error checking of pName left out */

pModule = PyImport_Import(pName);
Py_DECREF(pName);

if (pModule != NULL) {
    pFunc = PyObject_GetAttrString(pModule, argv[2]);
    /* pFunc is a new reference */

    if (pFunc && PyCallable_Check(pFunc)) {
        pArgs = PyTuple_New(argc - 3);
        for (i = 0; i < argc - 3; ++i) {
            pValue = PyInt_FromLong(atoi(argv[i + 3]));
            if (!pValue) {
                Py_DECREF(pArgs);
                Py_DECREF(pModule);
                fprintf(stderr, "Cannot convert argument\n");
                return 1;
            }
            /* pValue reference stolen here: */
            PyTuple_SetItem(pArgs, i, pValue);
        }
        pValue = PyObject_CallObject(pFunc, pArgs);
        Py_DECREF(pArgs);
        if (pValue != NULL) {
            printf("Result of call: %ld\n", PyInt_AsLong(pValue));
            Py_DECREF(pValue);
        }
        else {
            Py_DECREF(pFunc);
            Py_DECREF(pModule);
            PyErr_Print();
            fprintf(stderr,"Call failed\n");
            return 1;
        }
    }
    else {
        if (PyErr_Occurred())
            PyErr_Print();
        fprintf(stderr, "Cannot find function \"%s\"\n", argv[2]);
    }
    Py_XDECREF(pFunc);
    Py_DECREF(pModule);
```

```
    }
    else {
        PyErr_Print();
        fprintf(stderr, "Failed to load \"%s\"\n", argv[1]);
        return 1;
    }
    Py_Finalize();
    return 0;
}
```

This code loads a Python script using `argv[1]`, and calls the function named in `argv[2]`. Its integer arguments are the other values of the `argv` array. If you compile and link this program (let's call the finished executable **call**), and use it to execute a Python script, such as:

```
def multiply(a,b):
    print "Will compute", a, "times", b
    c = 0
    for i in range(0, a):
        c = c + b
    return c
```

then the result should be:

```
$ call multiply multiply 3 2
Will compute 3 times 2
Result of call: 6
```

Although the program is quite large for its functionality, most of the code is for data conversion between Python and C, and for error reporting. The interesting part with respect to embedding Python starts with

```
Py_Initialize();
pName = PyString_FromString(argv[1]);
/* Error checking of pName left out */
pModule = PyImport_Import(pName);
```

After initializing the interpreter, the script is loaded using `PyImport_Import()`. This routine needs a Python string as its argument, which is constructed using the `PyString_FromString()` data conversion routine.

```
pFunc = PyObject_GetAttrString(pModule, argv[2]);
/* pFunc is a new reference */

if (pFunc && PyCallable_Check(pFunc)) {
    ...
}
Py_XDECREF(pFunc);
```

Once the script is loaded, the name we're looking for is retrieved using `PyObject_GetAttrString()`. If the name exists, and the object returned is callable, you can safely assume that it is a function. The program then proceeds by constructing a tuple of arguments as normal. The call to the Python function is then made with:

```
pValue = PyObject_CallObject(pFunc, pArgs);
```

Upon return of the function, `pValue` is either *NULL* or it contains a reference to the return value of the function. Be sure to release the reference after examining the value.

5.4 Extending Embedded Python

Until now, the embedded Python interpreter had no access to functionality from the application itself. The Python API allows this by extending the embedded interpreter. That is, the embedded interpreter gets extended with routines provided by the application. While it sounds complex, it is not so bad. Simply forget for a while that the application starts the Python interpreter. Instead, consider the application to be a set of subroutines, and write some glue code that gives Python access to those routines, just like you would write a normal Python extension. For example:

```c
static int numargs=0;

/* Return the number of arguments of the application command line */
static PyObject*
emb_numargs(PyObject *self, PyObject *args)
{
    if(!PyArg_ParseTuple(args, ":numargs"))
        return NULL;
    return Py_BuildValue("i", numargs);
}

static PyMethodDef EmbMethods[] = {
    {"numargs", emb_numargs, METH_VARARGS,
     "Return the number of arguments received by the process."},
    {NULL, NULL, 0, NULL}
};
```

Insert the above code just above the `main()` function. Also, insert the following two statements directly after `Py_Initialize()`:

```c
numargs = argc;
Py_InitModule("emb", EmbMethods);
```

These two lines initialize the `numargs` variable, and make the `emb.numargs()` function accessible to the embedded Python interpreter. With these extensions, the Python script can do things like

```python
import emb
print "Number of arguments", emb.numargs()
```

In a real application, the methods will expose an API of the application to Python.

5.5 Embedding Python in C++

It is also possible to embed Python in a C++ program; precisely how this is done will depend on the details of the C++ system used; in general you will need to write the main program in C++, and use the C++ compiler to compile and link your program. There is no need to recompile Python itself using C++.

5.6 Compiling and Linking under Unix-like systems

It is not necessarily trivial to find the right flags to pass to your compiler (and linker) in order to embed the Python interpreter into your application, particularly because Python needs to load library modules implemented as C dynamic extensions (`.so` files) linked against it.

To find out the required compiler and linker flags, you can execute the `pythonX.Y-config` script which is generated as part of the installation process (a `python-config` script may also be available). This script has several options, of which the following will be directly useful to you:

- `pythonX.Y-config --cflags` will give you the recommended flags when compiling:

```
$ /opt/bin/python2.7-config --cflags
-I/opt/include/python2.7 -fno-strict-aliasing -DNDEBUG -g -fwrapv -O3 -Wall -Wstr
```

- `pythonX.Y-config --ldflags` will give you the recommended flags when linking:

```
$ /opt/bin/python2.7-config --ldflags
-L/opt/lib/python2.7/config -lpthread -ldl -lutil -lm -lpython2.7 -Xlinker -expor
```

Note: To avoid confusion between several Python installations (and especially between the system Python and your own compiled Python), it is recommended that you use the absolute path to `pythonX.Y-config`, as in the above example.

If this procedure doesn't work for you (it is not guaranteed to work for all Unix-like platforms; however, we welcome *bug reports*) you will have to read your system's documentation about dynamic linking and/or examine Python's `Makefile` (use `sysconfig.get_makefile_filename()` to find its location) and compilation options. In this case, the `sysconfig` module is a useful tool to programmatically extract the configuration values that you will want to combine together. For example:

```
>>> import sysconfig
>>> sysconfig.get_config_var('LIBS')
'-lpthread -ldl  -lutil'
>>> sysconfig.get_config_var('LINKFORSHARED')
'-Xlinker -export-dynamic'
```

GLOSSARY

`>>>` The default Python prompt of the interactive shell. Often seen for code examples which can be executed interactively in the interpreter.

`...` The default Python prompt of the interactive shell when entering code for an indented code block or within a pair of matching left and right delimiters (parentheses, square brackets or curly braces).

2to3 A tool that tries to convert Python 2.x code to Python 3.x code by handling most of the incompatibilities which can be detected by parsing the source and traversing the parse tree.

2to3 is available in the standard library as `lib2to3`; a standalone entry point is provided as `Tools/scripts/2to3`. See *2to3-reference*.

abstract base class Abstract base classes complement *duck-typing* by providing a way to define interfaces when other techniques like `hasattr()` would be clumsy or subtly wrong (for example with *magic methods*). ABCs introduce virtual subclasses, which are classes that don't inherit from a class but are still recognized by `isinstance()` and `issubclass()`; see the `abc` module documentation. Python comes with many built-in ABCs for data structures (in the `collections` module), numbers (in the `numbers` module), and streams (in the `io` module). You can create your own ABCs with the `abc` module.

argument A value passed to a *function* (or *method*) when calling the function. There are two types of arguments:

- *keyword argument*: an argument preceded by an identifier (e.g. `name=`) in a function call or passed as a value in a dictionary preceded by `**`. For example, 3 and 5 are both keyword arguments in the following calls to `complex()`:

```
complex(real=3, imag=5)
complex(**{'real': 3, 'imag': 5})
```

- *positional argument*: an argument that is not a keyword argument. Positional arguments can appear at the beginning of an argument list and/or be passed as elements of an *iterable* preceded by `*`. For example, 3 and 5 are both positional arguments in the following calls:

```
complex(3, 5)
complex(*(3, 5))
```

Arguments are assigned to the named local variables in a function body. See the *calls* section for the rules governing this assignment. Syntactically, any expression can be used to represent an argument; the evaluated value is assigned to the local variable.

See also the *parameter* glossary entry and the FAQ question on *the difference between arguments and parameters*.

attribute A value associated with an object which is referenced by name using dotted expressions. For example, if an object *o* has an attribute *a* it would be referenced as *o.a*.

BDFL Benevolent Dictator For Life, a.k.a. Guido van Rossum, Python's creator.

bytes-like object An object that supports the *buffer protocol*, like `str`, `bytearray` or `memoryview`. Bytes-like objects can be used for various operations that expect binary data, such as compression, saving to a binary file or sending over a socket. Some operations need the binary data to be mutable, in which case not all bytes-like objects can apply.

bytecode Python source code is compiled into bytecode, the internal representation of a Python program in the CPython interpreter. The bytecode is also cached in `.pyc` and `.pyo` files so that executing the same file is faster the second time (recompilation from source to bytecode can be avoided). This "intermediate language" is said to run on a *virtual machine* that executes the machine code corresponding to each bytecode. Do note that bytecodes are not expected to work between different Python virtual machines, nor to be stable between Python releases.

A list of bytecode instructions can be found in the documentation for *the dis module*.

class A template for creating user-defined objects. Class definitions normally contain method definitions which operate on instances of the class.

classic class Any class which does not inherit from `object`. See *new-style class*. Classic classes have been removed in Python 3.

coercion The implicit conversion of an instance of one type to another during an operation which involves two arguments of the same type. For example, `int(3.15)` converts the floating point number to the integer 3, but in 3+4.5, each argument is of a different type (one int, one float), and both must be converted to the same type before they can be added or it will raise a `TypeError`. Coercion between two operands can be performed with the `coerce` built-in function; thus, 3+4.5 is equivalent to calling `operator.add(*coerce(3, 4.5))` and results in `operator.add(3.0, 4.5)`. Without coercion, all arguments of even compatible types would have to be normalized to the same value by the programmer, e.g., `float(3)+4.5` rather than just 3+4.5.

complex number An extension of the familiar real number system in which all numbers are expressed as a sum of a real part and an imaginary part. Imaginary numbers are real multiples of the imaginary unit (the square root of -1), often written i in mathematics or j in engineering. Python has built-in support for complex numbers, which are written with this latter notation; the imaginary part is written with a j suffix, e.g., `3+1j`. To get access to complex equivalents of the `math` module, use `cmath`. Use of complex numbers is a fairly advanced mathematical feature. If you're not aware of a need for them, it's almost certain you can safely ignore them.

context manager An object which controls the environment seen in a `with` statement by defining `__enter__()` and `__exit__()` methods. See **PEP 343**.

CPython The canonical implementation of the Python programming language, as distributed on python.org. The term "CPython" is used when necessary to distinguish this implementation from others such as Jython or IronPython.

decorator A function returning another function, usually applied as a function transformation using the `@wrapper` syntax. Common examples for decorators are `classmethod()` and `staticmethod()`.

The decorator syntax is merely syntactic sugar, the following two function definitions are semantically equivalent:

```
def f(...):
    ...
f = staticmethod(f)

@staticmethod
def f(...):
    ...
```

The same concept exists for classes, but is less commonly used there. See the documentation for *function definitions* and *class definitions* for more about decorators.

descriptor Any *new-style* object which defines the methods __get__(), __set__(), or __delete__(). When a class attribute is a descriptor, its special binding behavior is triggered upon attribute lookup. Normally, using *a.b* to get, set or delete an attribute looks up the object named *b* in the class dictionary for *a*, but if *b* is a descriptor, the respective descriptor method gets called. Understanding descriptors is a key to a deep understanding of Python because they are the basis for many features including functions, methods, properties, class methods, static methods, and reference to super classes.

For more information about descriptors' methods, see *descriptors*.

dictionary An associative array, where arbitrary keys are mapped to values. The keys can be any object with __hash__() and __eq__() methods. Called a hash in Perl.

dictionary view The objects returned from dict.viewkeys(), dict.viewvalues(), and dict.viewitems() are called dictionary views. They provide a dynamic view on the dictionary's entries, which means that when the dictionary changes, the view reflects these changes. To force the dictionary view to become a full list use list(dictview). See *dict-views*.

docstring A string literal which appears as the first expression in a class, function or module. While ignored when the suite is executed, it is recognized by the compiler and put into the __doc__ attribute of the enclosing class, function or module. Since it is available via introspection, it is the canonical place for documentation of the object.

duck-typing A programming style which does not look at an object's type to determine if it has the right interface; instead, the method or attribute is simply called or used ("If it looks like a duck and quacks like a duck, it must be a duck.") By emphasizing interfaces rather than specific types, well-designed code improves its flexibility by allowing polymorphic substitution. Duck-typing avoids tests using type() or isinstance(). (Note, however, that duck-typing can be complemented with *abstract base classes*.) Instead, it typically employs hasattr() tests or *EAFP* programming.

EAFP Easier to ask for forgiveness than permission. This common Python coding style assumes the existence of valid keys or attributes and catches exceptions if the assumption proves false. This clean and fast style is characterized by the presence of many try and except statements. The technique contrasts with the *LBYL* style common to many other languages such as C.

expression A piece of syntax which can be evaluated to some value. In other words, an expression is an accumulation of expression elements like literals, names, attribute access, operators or function calls which all return a value. In contrast to many other languages, not all language constructs are expressions. There are also *statements* which cannot be used as expressions, such as print or if. Assignments are also statements, not expressions.

extension module A module written in C or C++, using Python's C API to interact with the core and with user code.

file object An object exposing a file-oriented API (with methods such as read() or write()) to an underlying resource. Depending on the way it was created, a file object can mediate access to a real on-disk file or to another type of storage or communication device (for example standard input/output, in-memory buffers, sockets, pipes, etc.). File objects are also called *file-like objects* or *streams*.

There are actually three categories of file objects: raw binary files, buffered binary files and text files. Their interfaces are defined in the io module. The canonical way to create a file object is by using the open() function.

file-like object A synonym for *file object*.

finder An object that tries to find the *loader* for a module. It must implement a method named find_module(). See **PEP 302** for details.

floor division Mathematical division that rounds down to nearest integer. The floor division operator is //. For example, the expression 11 // 4 evaluates to 2 in contrast to the 2.75 returned by float true division. Note that (-11) // 4 is -3 because that is -2.75 rounded *downward*. See **PEP 238**.

function A series of statements which returns some value to a caller. It can also be passed zero or more *arguments* which may be used in the execution of the body. See also *parameter*, *method*, and the *function* section.

__future__ A pseudo-module which programmers can use to enable new language features which are not compatible with the current interpreter. For example, the expression `11/4` currently evaluates to `2`. If the module in which it is executed had enabled *true division* by executing:

```
from __future__ import division
```

the expression `11/4` would evaluate to `2.75`. By importing the __future__ module and evaluating its variables, you can see when a new feature was first added to the language and when it will become the default:

```
>>> import __future__
>>> __future__.division
_Feature((2, 2, 0, 'alpha', 2), (3, 0, 0, 'alpha', 0), 8192)
```

garbage collection The process of freeing memory when it is not used anymore. Python performs garbage collection via reference counting and a cyclic garbage collector that is able to detect and break reference cycles.

generator A function which returns an iterator. It looks like a normal function except that it contains `yield` statements for producing a series of values usable in a for-loop or that can be retrieved one at a time with the `next()` function. Each `yield` temporarily suspends processing, remembering the location execution state (including local variables and pending try-statements). When the generator resumes, it picks-up where it left-off (in contrast to functions which start fresh on every invocation).

generator expression An expression that returns an iterator. It looks like a normal expression followed by a `for` expression defining a loop variable, range, and an optional `if` expression. The combined expression generates values for an enclosing function:

```
>>> sum(i*i for i in range(10))          # sum of squares 0, 1, 4, ... 81
285
```

GIL See *global interpreter lock*.

global interpreter lock The mechanism used by the *CPython* interpreter to assure that only one thread executes Python *bytecode* at a time. This simplifies the CPython implementation by making the object model (including critical built-in types such as `dict`) implicitly safe against concurrent access. Locking the entire interpreter makes it easier for the interpreter to be multi-threaded, at the expense of much of the parallelism afforded by multi-processor machines.

However, some extension modules, either standard or third-party, are designed so as to release the GIL when doing computationally-intensive tasks such as compression or hashing. Also, the GIL is always released when doing I/O.

Past efforts to create a "free-threaded" interpreter (one which locks shared data at a much finer granularity) have not been successful because performance suffered in the common single-processor case. It is believed that overcoming this performance issue would make the implementation much more complicated and therefore costlier to maintain.

hashable An object is *hashable* if it has a hash value which never changes during its lifetime (it needs a __hash__() method), and can be compared to other objects (it needs an __eq__() or __cmp__() method). Hashable objects which compare equal must have the same hash value.

Hashability makes an object usable as a dictionary key and a set member, because these data structures use the hash value internally.

All of Python's immutable built-in objects are hashable, while no mutable containers (such as lists or dictionaries) are. Objects which are instances of user-defined classes are hashable by default; they all compare unequal (except with themselves), and their hash value is their `id()`.

IDLE An Integrated Development Environment for Python. IDLE is a basic editor and interpreter environment which ships with the standard distribution of Python.

immutable   An object with a fixed value. Immutable objects include numbers, strings and tuples. Such an object cannot be altered. A new object has to be created if a different value has to be stored. They play an important role in places where a constant hash value is needed, for example as a key in a dictionary.

integer division   Mathematical division discarding any remainder. For example, the expression `11/4` currently evaluates to `2` in contrast to the `2.75` returned by float division. Also called *floor division*. When dividing two integers the outcome will always be another integer (having the floor function applied to it). However, if one of the operands is another numeric type (such as a `float`), the result will be coerced (see *coercion*) to a common type. For example, an integer divided by a float will result in a float value, possibly with a decimal fraction. Integer division can be forced by using the `//` operator instead of the `/` operator. See also *__future__*.

importing   The process by which Python code in one module is made available to Python code in another module.

importer   An object that both finds and loads a module; both a *finder* and *loader* object.

interactive   Python has an interactive interpreter which means you can enter statements and expressions at the interpreter prompt, immediately execute them and see their results. Just launch `python` with no arguments (possibly by selecting it from your computer's main menu). It is a very powerful way to test out new ideas or inspect modules and packages (remember `help(x)`).

interpreted   Python is an interpreted language, as opposed to a compiled one, though the distinction can be blurry because of the presence of the bytecode compiler. This means that source files can be run directly without explicitly creating an executable which is then run. Interpreted languages typically have a shorter development/debug cycle than compiled ones, though their programs generally also run more slowly. See also *interactive*.

iterable   An object capable of returning its members one at a time. Examples of iterables include all sequence types (such as `list`, `str`, and `tuple`) and some non-sequence types like `dict` and `file` and objects of any classes you define with an `__iter__()` or `__getitem__()` method. Iterables can be used in a `for` loop and in many other places where a sequence is needed (`zip()`, `map()`, ...). When an iterable object is passed as an argument to the built-in function `iter()`, it returns an iterator for the object. This iterator is good for one pass over the set of values. When using iterables, it is usually not necessary to call `iter()` or deal with iterator objects yourself. The `for` statement does that automatically for you, creating a temporary unnamed variable to hold the iterator for the duration of the loop. See also *iterator*, *sequence*, and *generator*.

iterator   An object representing a stream of data. Repeated calls to the iterator's `next()` method return successive items in the stream. When no more data are available a `StopIteration` exception is raised instead. At this point, the iterator object is exhausted and any further calls to its `next()` method just raise `StopIteration` again. Iterators are required to have an `__iter__()` method that returns the iterator object itself so every iterator is also iterable and may be used in most places where other iterables are accepted. One notable exception is code which attempts multiple iteration passes. A container object (such as a `list`) produces a fresh new iterator each time you pass it to the `iter()` function or use it in a `for` loop. Attempting this with an iterator will just return the same exhausted iterator object used in the previous iteration pass, making it appear like an empty container.

More information can be found in *typeiter*.

key function   A key function or collation function is a callable that returns a value used for sorting or ordering. For example, `locale.strxfrm()` is used to produce a sort key that is aware of locale specific sort conventions.

A number of tools in Python accept key functions to control how elements are ordered or grouped. They include `min()`, `max()`, `sorted()`, `list.sort()`, `heapq.nsmallest()`, `heapq.nlargest()`, and `itertools.groupby()`.

There are several ways to create a key function. For example. the `str.lower()` method can serve as a key function for case insensitive sorts. Alternatively, an ad-hoc key function can be built from a `lambda` expression such as `lambda r:  (r[0], r[2])`. Also, the `operator` module provides three key function constructors: `attrgetter()`, `itemgetter()`, and `methodcaller()`. See the *Sorting HOW TO* for examples of how to create and use key functions.

keyword argument   See *argument*.

lambda An anonymous inline function consisting of a single *expression* which is evaluated when the function is called. The syntax to create a lambda function is `lambda [arguments]: expression`

LBYL Look before you leap. This coding style explicitly tests for pre-conditions before making calls or lookups. This style contrasts with the *EAFP* approach and is characterized by the presence of many `if` statements.

In a multi-threaded environment, the LBYL approach can risk introducing a race condition between "the looking" and "the leaping". For example, the code, `if key in mapping: return mapping[key]` can fail if another thread removes *key* from *mapping* after the test, but before the lookup. This issue can be solved with locks or by using the EAFP approach.

list A built-in Python *sequence*. Despite its name it is more akin to an array in other languages than to a linked list since access to elements are O(1).

list comprehension A compact way to process all or part of the elements in a sequence and return a list with the results. `result = ["0x%02x" % x for x in range(256) if x % 2 == 0]` generates a list of strings containing even hex numbers (0x..) in the range from 0 to 255. The `if` clause is optional. If omitted, all elements in `range(256)` are processed.

loader An object that loads a module. It must define a method named `load_module()`. A loader is typically returned by a *finder*. See **PEP 302** for details.

mapping A container object that supports arbitrary key lookups and implements the methods specified in the `Mapping` or `MutableMapping` *abstract base classes*. Examples include `dict`, `collections.defaultdict`, `collections.OrderedDict` and `collections.Counter`.

metaclass The class of a class. Class definitions create a class name, a class dictionary, and a list of base classes. The metaclass is responsible for taking those three arguments and creating the class. Most object oriented programming languages provide a default implementation. What makes Python special is that it is possible to create custom metaclasses. Most users never need this tool, but when the need arises, metaclasses can provide powerful, elegant solutions. They have been used for logging attribute access, adding thread-safety, tracking object creation, implementing singletons, and many other tasks.

More information can be found in *metaclasses*.

method A function which is defined inside a class body. If called as an attribute of an instance of that class, the method will get the instance object as its first *argument* (which is usually called `self`). See *function* and *nested scope*.

method resolution order Method Resolution Order is the order in which base classes are searched for a member during lookup. See The Python 2.3 Method Resolution Order.

module An object that serves as an organizational unit of Python code. Modules have a namespace containing arbitrary Python objects. Modules are loaded into Python by the process of *importing*.

See also *package*.

MRO See *method resolution order*.

mutable Mutable objects can change their value but keep their `id()`. See also *immutable*.

named tuple Any tuple-like class whose indexable elements are also accessible using named attributes (for example, `time.localtime()` returns a tuple-like object where the *year* is accessible either with an index such as `t[0]` or with a named attribute like `t.tm_year`).

A named tuple can be a built-in type such as `time.struct_time`, or it can be created with a regular class definition. A full featured named tuple can also be created with the factory function `collections.namedtuple()`. The latter approach automatically provides extra features such as a self-documenting representation like `Employee(name='jones', title='programmer')`.

namespace The place where a variable is stored. Namespaces are implemented as dictionaries. There are the local, global and built-in namespaces as well as nested namespaces in objects (in methods). Namespaces support modularity by preventing naming conflicts. For instance, the functions `__builtin__.open()` and `os.open()` are distinguished by their namespaces. Namespaces also aid readability and maintainability by making it clear which module implements a function. For instance, writing `random.seed()` or `itertools.izip()` makes it clear that those functions are implemented by the `random` and `itertools` modules, respectively.

nested scope The ability to refer to a variable in an enclosing definition. For instance, a function defined inside another function can refer to variables in the outer function. Note that nested scopes work only for reference and not for assignment which will always write to the innermost scope. In contrast, local variables both read and write in the innermost scope. Likewise, global variables read and write to the global namespace.

new-style class Any class which inherits from `object`. This includes all built-in types like `list` and `dict`. Only new-style classes can use Python's newer, versatile features like `__slots__`, descriptors, properties, and `__getattribute__()`.

More information can be found in *newstyle*.

object Any data with state (attributes or value) and defined behavior (methods). Also the ultimate base class of any *new-style class*.

package A Python *module* which can contain submodules or recursively, subpackages. Technically, a package is a Python module with an `__path__` attribute.

parameter A named entity in a *function* (or method) definition that specifies an *argument* (or in some cases, arguments) that the function can accept. There are four types of parameters:

- *positional-or-keyword*: specifies an argument that can be passed either *positionally* or as a *keyword argument*. This is the default kind of parameter, for example *foo* and *bar* in the following:

  ```
  def func(foo, bar=None): ...
  ```

- *positional-only*: specifies an argument that can be supplied only by position. Python has no syntax for defining positional-only parameters. However, some built-in functions have positional-only parameters (e.g. `abs()`).

- *var-positional*: specifies that an arbitrary sequence of positional arguments can be provided (in addition to any positional arguments already accepted by other parameters). Such a parameter can be defined by prepending the parameter name with `*`, for example *args* in the following:

  ```
  def func(*args, **kwargs): ...
  ```

- *var-keyword*: specifies that arbitrarily many keyword arguments can be provided (in addition to any keyword arguments already accepted by other parameters). Such a parameter can be defined by prepending the parameter name with `**`, for example *kwargs* in the example above.

Parameters can specify both optional and required arguments, as well as default values for some optional arguments.

See also the *argument* glossary entry, the FAQ question on *the difference between arguments and parameters*, and the *function* section.

positional argument See *argument*.

Python 3000 Nickname for the Python 3.x release line (coined long ago when the release of version 3 was something in the distant future.) This is also abbreviated "Py3k".

Pythonic An idea or piece of code which closely follows the most common idioms of the Python language, rather than implementing code using concepts common to other languages. For example, a common idiom in Python is to loop over all elements of an iterable using a `for` statement. Many other languages don't have this type of construct, so people unfamiliar with Python sometimes use a numerical counter instead:

```
for i in range(len(food)):
    print food[i]
```

As opposed to the cleaner, Pythonic method:

```
for piece in food:
    print piece
```

reference count   The number of references to an object. When the reference count of an object drops to zero, it is deallocated. Reference counting is generally not visible to Python code, but it is a key element of the *CPython* implementation. The sys module defines a getrefcount() function that programmers can call to return the reference count for a particular object.

__slots__   A declaration inside a *new-style class* that saves memory by pre-declaring space for instance attributes and eliminating instance dictionaries. Though popular, the technique is somewhat tricky to get right and is best reserved for rare cases where there are large numbers of instances in a memory-critical application.

sequence   An *iterable* which supports efficient element access using integer indices via the __getitem__() special method and defines a len() method that returns the length of the sequence. Some built-in sequence types are list, str, tuple, and unicode. Note that dict also supports __getitem__() and __len__(), but is considered a mapping rather than a sequence because the lookups use arbitrary *immutable* keys rather than integers.

slice   An object usually containing a portion of a *sequence*. A slice is created using the subscript notation, [] with colons between numbers when several are given, such as in variable_name[1:3:5]. The bracket (subscript) notation uses slice objects internally (or in older versions, __getslice__() and __setslice__()).

special method   A method that is called implicitly by Python to execute a certain operation on a type, such as addition. Such methods have names starting and ending with double underscores. Special methods are documented in *specialnames*.

statement   A statement is part of a suite (a "block" of code). A statement is either an *expression* or one of several constructs with a keyword, such as if, while or for.

struct sequence   A tuple with named elements. Struct sequences expose an interface similiar to *named tuple* in that elements can either be accessed either by index or as an attribute. However, they do not have any of the named tuple methods like _make() or _asdict(). Examples of struct sequences include sys.float_info and the return value of os.stat().

triple-quoted string   A string which is bound by three instances of either a quotation mark (") or an apostrophe ('). While they don't provide any functionality not available with single-quoted strings, they are useful for a number of reasons. They allow you to include unescaped single and double quotes within a string and they can span multiple lines without the use of the continuation character, making them especially useful when writing docstrings.

type   The type of a Python object determines what kind of object it is; every object has a type. An object's type is accessible as its __class__ attribute or can be retrieved with type(obj).

universal newlines   A manner of interpreting text streams in which all of the following are recognized as ending a line: the Unix end-of-line convention '\n', the Windows convention '\r\n', and the old Macintosh convention '\r'. See PEP 278 and PEP 3116, as well as str.splitlines() for an additional use.

virtual environment   A cooperatively isolated runtime environment that allows Python users and applications to install and upgrade Python distribution packages without interfering with the behaviour of other Python applications running on the same system.

virtual machine   A computer defined entirely in software. Python's virtual machine executes the *bytecode* emitted by the bytecode compiler.

Zen of Python   Listing of Python design principles and philosophies that are helpful in understanding and using the language. The listing can be found by typing "import this" at the interactive prompt.

ABOUT THESE DOCUMENTS

These documents are generated from reStructuredText sources by Sphinx, a document processor specifically written for the Python documentation.

Development of the documentation and its toolchain is an entirely volunteer effort, just like Python itself. If you want to contribute, please take a look at the *reporting-bugs* page for information on how to do so. New volunteers are always welcome!

Many thanks go to:

- Fred L. Drake, Jr., the creator of the original Python documentation toolset and writer of much of the content;

- the Docutils project for creating reStructuredText and the Docutils suite;

- Fredrik Lundh for his Alternative Python Reference project from which Sphinx got many good ideas.

B.1 Contributors to the Python Documentation

Many people have contributed to the Python language, the Python standard library, and the Python documentation. See Misc/ACKS in the Python source distribution for a partial list of contributors.

It is only with the input and contributions of the Python community that Python has such wonderful documentation – Thank You!

Appendix B. About these documents

HISTORY AND LICENSE

C.1 History of the software

Python was created in the early 1990s by Guido van Rossum at Stichting Mathematisch Centrum (CWI, see http://www.cwi.nl/) in the Netherlands as a successor of a language called ABC. Guido remains Python's principal author, although it includes many contributions from others.

In 1995, Guido continued his work on Python at the Corporation for National Research Initiatives (CNRI, see http://www.cnri.reston.va.us/) in Reston, Virginia where he released several versions of the software.

In May 2000, Guido and the Python core development team moved to BeOpen.com to form the BeOpen Python-Labs team. In October of the same year, the PythonLabs team moved to Digital Creations (now Zope Corporation; see http://www.zope.com/). In 2001, the Python Software Foundation (PSF, see https://www.python.org/psf/) was formed, a non-profit organization created specifically to own Python-related Intellectual Property. Zope Corporation is a sponsoring member of the PSF.

All Python releases are Open Source (see http://opensource.org/ for the Open Source Definition). Historically, most, but not all, Python releases have also been GPL-compatible; the table below summarizes the various releases.

Release	Derived from	Year	Owner	GPL compatible?
0.9.0 thru 1.2	n/a	1991-1995	CWI	yes
1.3 thru 1.5.2	1.2	1995-1999	CNRI	yes
1.6	1.5.2	2000	CNRI	no
2.0	1.6	2000	BeOpen.com	no
1.6.1	1.6	2001	CNRI	no
2.1	2.0+1.6.1	2001	PSF	no
2.0.1	2.0+1.6.1	2001	PSF	yes
2.1.1	2.1+2.0.1	2001	PSF	yes
2.1.2	2.1.1	2002	PSF	yes
2.1.3	2.1.2	2002	PSF	yes
2.2 and above	2.1.1	2001-now	PSF	yes

Note: GPL-compatible doesn't mean that we're distributing Python under the GPL. All Python licenses, unlike the GPL, let you distribute a modified version without making your changes open source. The GPL-compatible licenses make it possible to combine Python with other software that is released under the GPL; the others don't.

Thanks to the many outside volunteers who have worked under Guido's direction to make these releases possible.

C.2 Terms and conditions for accessing or otherwise using Python

PSF LICENSE AGREEMENT FOR PYTHON 2.7.10

1. This LICENSE AGREEMENT is between the Python Software Foundation ("PSF"), and the Individual or Organization ("Licensee") accessing and otherwise using Python 2.7.10 software in source or binary form and its associated documentation.

2. Subject to the terms and conditions of this License Agreement, PSF hereby grants Licensee a nonexclusive, royalty-free, world-wide license to reproduce, analyze, test, perform and/or display publicly, prepare derivative works, distribute, and otherwise use Python 2.7.10 alone or in any derivative version, provided, however, that PSF's License Agreement and PSF's notice of copyright, i.e., "Copyright © 2001-2015 Python Software Foundation; All Rights Reserved" are retained in Python 2.7.10 alone or in any derivative version prepared by Licensee.

3. In the event Licensee prepares a derivative work that is based on or incorporates Python 2.7.10 or any part thereof, and wants to make the derivative work available to others as provided herein, then Licensee hereby agrees to include in any such work a brief summary of the changes made to Python 2.7.10.

4. PSF is making Python 2.7.10 available to Licensee on an "AS IS" basis. PSF MAKES NO REPRESENTATIONS OR WARRANTIES, EXPRESS OR IMPLIED. BY WAY OF EXAMPLE, BUT NOT LIMITATION, PSF MAKES NO AND DISCLAIMS ANY REPRESENTATION OR WARRANTY OF MERCHANTABILITY OR FITNESS FOR ANY PARTICULAR PURPOSE OR THAT THE USE OF PYTHON 2.7.10 WILL NOT INFRINGE ANY THIRD PARTY RIGHTS.

5. PSF SHALL NOT BE LIABLE TO LICENSEE OR ANY OTHER USERS OF PYTHON 2.7.10 FOR ANY INCIDENTAL, SPECIAL, OR CONSEQUENTIAL DAMAGES OR LOSS AS A RESULT OF MODIFYING, DISTRIBUTING, OR OTHERWISE USING PYTHON 2.7.10, OR ANY DERIVATIVE THEREOF, EVEN IF ADVISED OF THE POSSIBILITY THEREOF.

6. This License Agreement will automatically terminate upon a material breach of its terms and conditions.

7. Nothing in this License Agreement shall be deemed to create any relationship of agency, partnership, or joint venture between PSF and Licensee. This License Agreement does not grant permission to use PSF trademarks or trade name in a trademark sense to endorse or promote products or services of Licensee, or any third party.

8. By copying, installing or otherwise using Python 2.7.10, Licensee agrees to be bound by the terms and conditions of this License Agreement.

BEOPEN.COM LICENSE AGREEMENT FOR PYTHON 2.0

BEOPEN PYTHON OPEN SOURCE LICENSE AGREEMENT VERSION 1

1. This LICENSE AGREEMENT is between BeOpen.com ("BeOpen"), having an office at 160 Saratoga Avenue, Santa Clara, CA 95051, and the Individual or Organization ("Licensee") accessing and otherwise using this software in source or binary form and its associated documentation ("the Software").

2. Subject to the terms and conditions of this BeOpen Python License Agreement, BeOpen hereby grants Licensee a non-exclusive, royalty-free, world-wide license to reproduce, analyze, test, perform and/or display publicly, prepare derivative works, distribute, and otherwise use the Software alone or in any derivative version, provided, however, that the BeOpen Python License is retained in the Software, alone or in any derivative version prepared by Licensee.

3. BeOpen is making the Software available to Licensee on an "AS IS" basis. BEOPEN MAKES NO REPRESENTATIONS OR WARRANTIES, EXPRESS OR IMPLIED. BY WAY OF EXAMPLE, BUT NOT LIMITATION, BEOPEN MAKES NO AND DISCLAIMS ANY REPRESENTATION OR WARRANTY OF MERCHANTABILITY OR FITNESS FOR ANY PARTICULAR PURPOSE OR THAT THE USE OF THE SOFTWARE WILL NOT INFRINGE ANY THIRD PARTY RIGHTS.

4. BEOPEN SHALL NOT BE LIABLE TO LICENSEE OR ANY OTHER USERS OF THE SOFTWARE FOR ANY INCIDENTAL, SPECIAL, OR CONSEQUENTIAL DAMAGES OR LOSS AS A RESULT OF USING, MODIFYING OR DISTRIBUTING THE SOFTWARE, OR ANY DERIVATIVE THEREOF, EVEN IF ADVISED OF THE POSSIBILITY THEREOF.

5. This License Agreement will automatically terminate upon a material breach of its terms and conditions.

6. This License Agreement shall be governed by and interpreted in all respects by the law of the State of California, excluding conflict of law provisions. Nothing in this License Agreement shall be deemed to create any relationship of agency, partnership, or joint venture between BeOpen and Licensee. This License Agreement does not grant permission to use BeOpen trademarks or trade names in a trademark sense to endorse or promote products or services of Licensee, or any third party. As an exception, the "BeOpen Python" logos available at http://www.pythonlabs.com/logos.html may be used according to the permissions granted on that web page.

7. By copying, installing or otherwise using the software, Licensee agrees to be bound by the terms and conditions of this License Agreement.

CNRI LICENSE AGREEMENT FOR PYTHON 1.6.1

1. This LICENSE AGREEMENT is between the Corporation for National Research Initiatives, having an office at 1895 Preston White Drive, Reston, VA 20191 ("CNRI"), and the Individual or Organization ("Licensee") accessing and otherwise using Python 1.6.1 software in source or binary form and its associated documentation.

2. Subject to the terms and conditions of this License Agreement, CNRI hereby grants Licensee a nonexclusive, royalty-free, world-wide license to reproduce, analyze, test, perform and/or display publicly, prepare derivative works, distribute, and otherwise use Python 1.6.1 alone or in any derivative version, provided, however, that CNRI's License Agreement and CNRI's notice of copyright, i.e., "Copyright © 1995-2001 Corporation for National Research Initiatives; All Rights Reserved" are retained in Python 1.6.1 alone or in any derivative version prepared by Licensee. Alternately, in lieu of CNRI's License Agreement, Licensee may substitute the following text (omitting the quotes): "Python 1.6.1 is made available subject to the terms and conditions in CNRI's License Agreement. This Agreement together with Python 1.6.1 may be located on the Internet using the following unique, persistent identifier (known as a handle): 1895.22/1013. This Agreement may also be obtained from a proxy server on the Internet using the following URL: http://hdl.handle.net/1895.22/1013."

3. In the event Licensee prepares a derivative work that is based on or incorporates Python 1.6.1 or any part thereof, and wants to make the derivative work available to others as provided herein, then Licensee hereby agrees to include in any such work a brief summary of the changes made to Python 1.6.1.

4. CNRI is making Python 1.6.1 available to Licensee on an "AS IS" basis. CNRI MAKES NO REPRESENTATIONS OR WARRANTIES, EXPRESS OR IMPLIED. BY WAY OF EXAMPLE, BUT NOT LIMITATION, CNRI MAKES NO AND DISCLAIMS ANY REPRESENTATION OR WARRANTY OF MERCHANTABILITY OR FITNESS FOR ANY PARTICULAR PURPOSE OR THAT THE USE OF PYTHON 1.6.1 WILL NOT INFRINGE ANY THIRD PARTY RIGHTS.

5. CNRI SHALL NOT BE LIABLE TO LICENSEE OR ANY OTHER USERS OF PYTHON 1.6.1 FOR ANY INCIDENTAL, SPECIAL, OR CONSEQUENTIAL DAMAGES OR LOSS AS A RESULT OF MODIFYING, DISTRIBUTING, OR OTHERWISE USING PYTHON 1.6.1, OR ANY DERIVATIVE THEREOF, EVEN IF ADVISED OF THE POSSIBILITY THEREOF.

6. This License Agreement will automatically terminate upon a material breach of its terms and conditions.

7. This License Agreement shall be governed by the federal intellectual property law of the United States, including without limitation the federal copyright law, and, to the extent such U.S. federal law does not apply, by the law of the Commonwealth of Virginia, excluding Virginia's conflict of law provisions. Notwithstanding the foregoing, with regard to derivative works based on Python 1.6.1 that incorporate non-separable material that was previously distributed under the GNU General Public License (GPL), the law of the Commonwealth of Virginia shall govern this License Agreement only as to issues arising under or with respect to Paragraphs 4, 5, and 7 of this License Agreement. Nothing in this License Agreement shall be deemed to create any relationship of agency, partnership, or joint venture between CNRI and Licensee. This License Agreement does not grant permission to use CNRI trademarks or trade name in a trademark sense to endorse or promote products or services of Licensee, or any third party.

8. By clicking on the "ACCEPT" button where indicated, or by copying, installing or otherwise using Python 1.6.1, Licensee agrees to be bound by the terms and conditions of this License Agreement.

ACCEPT

C.3 Licenses and Acknowledgements for Incorporated Software

This section is an incomplete, but growing list of licenses and acknowledgements for third-party software incorporated in the Python distribution.

C.3.1 Mersenne Twister

The _random module includes code based on a download from http://www.math.sci.hiroshima-u.ac.jp/~m-mat/MT/MT2002/emt19937ar.html. The following are the verbatim comments from the original code:

```
A C-program for MT19937, with initialization improved 2002/1/26.
Coded by Takuji Nishimura and Makoto Matsumoto.

Before using, initialize the state by using init_genrand(seed)
or init_by_array(init_key, key_length).

Copyright (C) 1997 - 2002, Makoto Matsumoto and Takuji Nishimura,
All rights reserved.

Redistribution and use in source and binary forms, with or without
modification, are permitted provided that the following conditions
are met:

  1. Redistributions of source code must retain the above copyright
     notice, this list of conditions and the following disclaimer.

  2. Redistributions in binary form must reproduce the above copyright
     notice, this list of conditions and the following disclaimer in the
     documentation and/or other materials provided with the distribution.

  3. The names of its contributors may not be used to endorse or promote
     products derived from this software without specific prior written
     permission.

THIS SOFTWARE IS PROVIDED BY THE COPYRIGHT HOLDERS AND CONTRIBUTORS
"AS IS" AND ANY EXPRESS OR IMPLIED WARRANTIES, INCLUDING, BUT NOT
```

```
LIMITED TO, THE IMPLIED WARRANTIES OF MERCHANTABILITY AND FITNESS FOR
A PARTICULAR PURPOSE ARE DISCLAIMED.  IN NO EVENT SHALL THE COPYRIGHT OWNER OR
CONTRIBUTORS BE LIABLE FOR ANY DIRECT, INDIRECT, INCIDENTAL, SPECIAL,
EXEMPLARY, OR CONSEQUENTIAL DAMAGES (INCLUDING, BUT NOT LIMITED TO,
PROCUREMENT OF SUBSTITUTE GOODS OR SERVICES; LOSS OF USE, DATA, OR
PROFITS; OR BUSINESS INTERRUPTION) HOWEVER CAUSED AND ON ANY THEORY OF
LIABILITY, WHETHER IN CONTRACT, STRICT LIABILITY, OR TORT (INCLUDING
NEGLIGENCE OR OTHERWISE) ARISING IN ANY WAY OUT OF THE USE OF THIS
SOFTWARE, EVEN IF ADVISED OF THE POSSIBILITY OF SUCH DAMAGE.


Any feedback is very welcome.
http://www.math.sci.hiroshima-u.ac.jp/~m-mat/MT/emt.html
email: m-mat @ math.sci.hiroshima-u.ac.jp (remove space)
```

C.3.2 Sockets

The socket module uses the functions, getaddrinfo(), and getnameinfo(), which are coded in separate source files from the WIDE Project, http://www.wide.ad.jp/.

```
Copyright (C) 1995, 1996, 1997, and 1998 WIDE Project.
All rights reserved.

Redistribution and use in source and binary forms, with or without
modification, are permitted provided that the following conditions
are met:
1. Redistributions of source code must retain the above copyright
   notice, this list of conditions and the following disclaimer.
2. Redistributions in binary form must reproduce the above copyright
   notice, this list of conditions and the following disclaimer in the
   documentation and/or other materials provided with the distribution.
3. Neither the name of the project nor the names of its contributors
   may be used to endorse or promote products derived from this software
   without specific prior written permission.

THIS SOFTWARE IS PROVIDED BY THE PROJECT AND CONTRIBUTORS ``AS IS'' AND
GAI_ANY EXPRESS OR IMPLIED WARRANTIES, INCLUDING, BUT NOT LIMITED TO, THE
IMPLIED WARRANTIES OF MERCHANTABILITY AND FITNESS FOR A PARTICULAR PURPOSE
ARE DISCLAIMED.  IN NO EVENT SHALL THE PROJECT OR CONTRIBUTORS BE LIABLE
FOR GAI_ANY DIRECT, INDIRECT, INCIDENTAL, SPECIAL, EXEMPLARY, OR CONSEQUENTIAL
DAMAGES (INCLUDING, BUT NOT LIMITED TO, PROCUREMENT OF SUBSTITUTE GOODS
OR SERVICES; LOSS OF USE, DATA, OR PROFITS; OR BUSINESS INTERRUPTION)
HOWEVER CAUSED AND ON GAI_ANY THEORY OF LIABILITY, WHETHER IN CONTRACT, STRICT
LIABILITY, OR TORT (INCLUDING NEGLIGENCE OR OTHERWISE) ARISING IN GAI_ANY WAY
OUT OF THE USE OF THIS SOFTWARE, EVEN IF ADVISED OF THE POSSIBILITY OF
SUCH DAMAGE.
```

C.3.3 Floating point exception control

The source for the fpectl module includes the following notice:

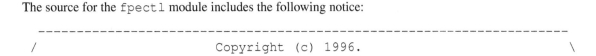

```
     ---------------------------------------------------------------------
    /                       Copyright (c) 1996.                          \
```

```
|          The Regents of the University of California.           |
|                     All rights reserved.                        |
|                                                                 |
|   Permission to use, copy, modify, and distribute this software for |
|   any purpose without fee is hereby granted, provided that this en- |
|   tire notice is included in all copies of any software which is or |
|   includes   a   copy  or  modification  of  this software and in all |
|   copies of the supporting documentation for such software.     |
|                                                                 |
|   This  work was produced at the University of California, Lawrence |
|   Livermore National Laboratory under  contract  no.  W-7405-ENG-48 |
|   between  the  U.S.  Department  of  Energy and The Regents of the |
|   University of California for the operation of UC LLNL.         |
|                                                                 |
|                          DISCLAIMER                             |
|                                                                 |
|   This  software was prepared as an account of work sponsored by an |
|   agency of the United States Government. Neither the United States |
|   Government  nor the University of California nor any of their em- |
|   ployees, makes any warranty, express or implied, or  assumes  any |
|   liability  or  responsibility  for the accuracy, completeness, or |
|   usefulness of any information,  apparatus,  product,  or  process |
|   disclosed,   or  represents  that  its  use  would  not  infringe |
|   privately-owned rights. Reference herein to any specific  commer- |
|   cial  products,  process,  or  service  by trade name, trademark, |
|   manufacturer, or otherwise, does not  necessarily  constitute  or |
|   imply  its endorsement, recommendation, or favoring by the United |
|   States Government or the University of California. The views  and |
|   opinions  of authors expressed herein do not necessarily state or |
|   reflect those of the United States Government or  the  University |
|   of  California,  and shall not be used for advertising or product |
\   endorsement purposes.                                          /
 -----------------------------------------------------------------
```

C.3.4 MD5 message digest algorithm

The source code for the md5 module contains the following notice:

```
Copyright (C) 1999, 2002 Aladdin Enterprises.  All rights reserved.

This software is provided 'as-is', without any express or implied
warranty.  In no event will the authors be held liable for any damages
arising from the use of this software.

Permission is granted to anyone to use this software for any purpose,
including commercial applications, and to alter it and redistribute it
freely, subject to the following restrictions:

1. The origin of this software must not be misrepresented; you must not
   claim that you wrote the original software. If you use this software
   in a product, an acknowledgment in the product documentation would be
   appreciated but is not required.
2. Altered source versions must be plainly marked as such, and must not be
   misrepresented as being the original software.
```

3. This notice may not be removed or altered from any source distribution.

L. Peter Deutsch
ghost@aladdin.com

Independent implementation of MD5 (RFC 1321).

This code implements the MD5 Algorithm defined in RFC 1321, whose
text is available at
        http://www.ietf.org/rfc/rfc1321.txt
The code is derived from the text of the RFC, including the test suite
(section A.5) but excluding the rest of Appendix A. It does not include
any code or documentation that is identified in the RFC as being
copyrighted.

The original and principal author of md5.h is L. Peter Deutsch
<ghost@aladdin.com>. Other authors are noted in the change history
that follows (in reverse chronological order):

2002-04-13 lpd Removed support for non-ANSI compilers; removed
        references to Ghostscript; clarified derivation from RFC 1321;
        now handles byte order either statically or dynamically.
1999-11-04 lpd Edited comments slightly for automatic TOC extraction.
1999-10-18 lpd Fixed typo in header comment (ansi2knr rather than md5);
        added conditionalization for C++ compilation from Martin
        Purschke <purschke@bnl.gov>.
1999-05-03 lpd Original version.

C.3.5 Asynchronous socket services

The asynchat and asyncore modules contain the following notice:

Copyright 1996 by Sam Rushing

                     All Rights Reserved

Permission to use, copy, modify, and distribute this software and
its documentation for any purpose and without fee is hereby
granted, provided that the above copyright notice appear in all
copies and that both that copyright notice and this permission
notice appear in supporting documentation, and that the name of Sam
Rushing not be used in advertising or publicity pertaining to
distribution of the software without specific, written prior
permission.

SAM RUSHING DISCLAIMS ALL WARRANTIES WITH REGARD TO THIS SOFTWARE,
INCLUDING ALL IMPLIED WARRANTIES OF MERCHANTABILITY AND FITNESS, IN
NO EVENT SHALL SAM RUSHING BE LIABLE FOR ANY SPECIAL, INDIRECT OR
CONSEQUENTIAL DAMAGES OR ANY DAMAGES WHATSOEVER RESULTING FROM LOSS
OF USE, DATA OR PROFITS, WHETHER IN AN ACTION OF CONTRACT,
NEGLIGENCE OR OTHER TORTIOUS ACTION, ARISING OUT OF OR IN
CONNECTION WITH THE USE OR PERFORMANCE OF THIS SOFTWARE.

C.3.6 Cookie management

The Cookie module contains the following notice:

```
Copyright 2000 by Timothy O'Malley <timo@alum.mit.edu>

                    All Rights Reserved

Permission to use, copy, modify, and distribute this software
and its documentation for any purpose and without fee is hereby
granted, provided that the above copyright notice appear in all
copies and that both that copyright notice and this permission
notice appear in supporting documentation, and that the name of
Timothy O'Malley  not be used in advertising or publicity
pertaining to distribution of the software without specific, written
prior permission.

Timothy O'Malley DISCLAIMS ALL WARRANTIES WITH REGARD TO THIS
SOFTWARE, INCLUDING ALL IMPLIED WARRANTIES OF MERCHANTABILITY
AND FITNESS, IN NO EVENT SHALL Timothy O'Malley BE LIABLE FOR
ANY SPECIAL, INDIRECT OR CONSEQUENTIAL DAMAGES OR ANY DAMAGES
WHATSOEVER RESULTING FROM LOSS OF USE, DATA OR PROFITS,
WHETHER IN AN ACTION OF CONTRACT, NEGLIGENCE OR OTHER TORTIOUS
ACTION, ARISING OUT OF OR IN CONNECTION WITH THE USE OR
PERFORMANCE OF THIS SOFTWARE.
```

C.3.7 Execution tracing

The trace module contains the following notice:

```
portions copyright 2001, Autonomous Zones Industries, Inc., all rights...
err...  reserved and offered to the public under the terms of the
Python 2.2 license.
Author: Zooko O'Whielacronx
http://zooko.com/
mailto:zooko@zooko.com

Copyright 2000, Mojam Media, Inc., all rights reserved.
Author: Skip Montanaro

Copyright 1999, Bioreason, Inc., all rights reserved.
Author: Andrew Dalke

Copyright 1995-1997, Automatrix, Inc., all rights reserved.
Author: Skip Montanaro

Copyright 1991-1995, Stichting Mathematisch Centrum, all rights reserved.


Permission to use, copy, modify, and distribute this Python software and
its associated documentation for any purpose without fee is hereby
granted, provided that the above copyright notice appears in all copies,
and that both that copyright notice and this permission notice appear in
supporting documentation, and that the name of neither Automatrix,
```

Bioreason or Mojam Media be used in advertising or publicity pertaining to
distribution of the software without specific, written prior permission.

C.3.8 UUencode and UUdecode functions

The uu module contains the following notice:

```
Copyright 1994 by Lance Ellinghouse
Cathedral City, California Republic, United States of America.
                    All Rights Reserved
Permission to use, copy, modify, and distribute this software and its
documentation for any purpose and without fee is hereby granted,
provided that the above copyright notice appear in all copies and that
both that copyright notice and this permission notice appear in
supporting documentation, and that the name of Lance Ellinghouse
not be used in advertising or publicity pertaining to distribution
of the software without specific, written prior permission.
LANCE ELLINGHOUSE DISCLAIMS ALL WARRANTIES WITH REGARD TO
THIS SOFTWARE, INCLUDING ALL IMPLIED WARRANTIES OF MERCHANTABILITY AND
FITNESS, IN NO EVENT SHALL LANCE ELLINGHOUSE CENTRUM BE LIABLE
FOR ANY SPECIAL, INDIRECT OR CONSEQUENTIAL DAMAGES OR ANY DAMAGES
WHATSOEVER RESULTING FROM LOSS OF USE, DATA OR PROFITS, WHETHER IN AN
ACTION OF CONTRACT, NEGLIGENCE OR OTHER TORTIOUS ACTION, ARISING OUT
OF OR IN CONNECTION WITH THE USE OR PERFORMANCE OF THIS SOFTWARE.

Modified by Jack Jansen, CWI, July 1995:
- Use binascii module to do the actual line-by-line conversion
  between ascii and binary. This results in a 1000-fold speedup. The C
  version is still 5 times faster, though.
- Arguments more compliant with Python standard
```

C.3.9 XML Remote Procedure Calls

The xmlrpclib module contains the following notice:

```
    The XML-RPC client interface is

Copyright (c) 1999-2002 by Secret Labs AB
Copyright (c) 1999-2002 by Fredrik Lundh

By obtaining, using, and/or copying this software and/or its
associated documentation, you agree that you have read, understood,
and will comply with the following terms and conditions:

Permission to use, copy, modify, and distribute this software and
its associated documentation for any purpose and without fee is
hereby granted, provided that the above copyright notice appears in
all copies, and that both that copyright notice and this permission
notice appear in supporting documentation, and that the name of
Secret Labs AB or the author not be used in advertising or publicity
pertaining to distribution of the software without specific, written
prior permission.
```

SECRET LABS AB AND THE AUTHOR DISCLAIMS ALL WARRANTIES WITH REGARD
TO THIS SOFTWARE, INCLUDING ALL IMPLIED WARRANTIES OF MERCHANT-
ABILITY AND FITNESS. IN NO EVENT SHALL SECRET LABS AB OR THE AUTHOR
BE LIABLE FOR ANY SPECIAL, INDIRECT OR CONSEQUENTIAL DAMAGES OR ANY
DAMAGES WHATSOEVER RESULTING FROM LOSS OF USE, DATA OR PROFITS,
WHETHER IN AN ACTION OF CONTRACT, NEGLIGENCE OR OTHER TORTIOUS
ACTION, ARISING OUT OF OR IN CONNECTION WITH THE USE OR PERFORMANCE
OF THIS SOFTWARE.

C.3.10 test_epoll

The `test_epoll` contains the following notice:

Copyright (c) 2001-2006 Twisted Matrix Laboratories.

Permission is hereby granted, free of charge, to any person obtaining
a copy of this software and associated documentation files (the
"Software"), to deal in the Software without restriction, including
without limitation the rights to use, copy, modify, merge, publish,
distribute, sublicense, and/or sell copies of the Software, and to
permit persons to whom the Software is furnished to do so, subject to
the following conditions:

The above copyright notice and this permission notice shall be
included in all copies or substantial portions of the Software.

THE SOFTWARE IS PROVIDED "AS IS", WITHOUT WARRANTY OF ANY KIND,
EXPRESS OR IMPLIED, INCLUDING BUT NOT LIMITED TO THE WARRANTIES OF
MERCHANTABILITY, FITNESS FOR A PARTICULAR PURPOSE AND
NONINFRINGEMENT. IN NO EVENT SHALL THE AUTHORS OR COPYRIGHT HOLDERS BE
LIABLE FOR ANY CLAIM, DAMAGES OR OTHER LIABILITY, WHETHER IN AN ACTION
OF CONTRACT, TORT OR OTHERWISE, ARISING FROM, OUT OF OR IN CONNECTION
WITH THE SOFTWARE OR THE USE OR OTHER DEALINGS IN THE SOFTWARE.

C.3.11 Select kqueue

The `select` and contains the following notice for the kqueue interface:

Copyright (c) 2000 Doug White, 2006 James Knight, 2007 Christian Heimes
All rights reserved.

Redistribution and use in source and binary forms, with or without
modification, are permitted provided that the following conditions
are met:
1. Redistributions of source code must retain the above copyright
   notice, this list of conditions and the following disclaimer.
2. Redistributions in binary form must reproduce the above copyright
   notice, this list of conditions and the following disclaimer in the
   documentation and/or other materials provided with the distribution.

THIS SOFTWARE IS PROVIDED BY THE AUTHOR AND CONTRIBUTORS ``AS IS'' AND
ANY EXPRESS OR IMPLIED WARRANTIES, INCLUDING, BUT NOT LIMITED TO, THE
IMPLIED WARRANTIES OF MERCHANTABILITY AND FITNESS FOR A PARTICULAR PURPOSE

```
ARE DISCLAIMED.  IN NO EVENT SHALL THE AUTHOR OR CONTRIBUTORS BE LIABLE
FOR ANY DIRECT, INDIRECT, INCIDENTAL, SPECIAL, EXEMPLARY, OR CONSEQUENTIAL
DAMAGES (INCLUDING, BUT NOT LIMITED TO, PROCUREMENT OF SUBSTITUTE GOODS
OR SERVICES; LOSS OF USE, DATA, OR PROFITS; OR BUSINESS INTERRUPTION)
HOWEVER CAUSED AND ON ANY THEORY OF LIABILITY, WHETHER IN CONTRACT, STRICT
LIABILITY, OR TORT (INCLUDING NEGLIGENCE OR OTHERWISE) ARISING IN ANY WAY
OUT OF THE USE OF THIS SOFTWARE, EVEN IF ADVISED OF THE POSSIBILITY OF
SUCH DAMAGE.
```

C.3.12 strtod and dtoa

The file `Python/dtoa.c`, which supplies C functions dtoa and strtod for conversion of C doubles to and from strings, is derived from the file of the same name by David M. Gay, currently available from http://www.netlib.org/fp/. The original file, as retrieved on March 16, 2009, contains the following copyright and licensing notice:

```
/**********************************************************************
 *
 * The author of this software is David M. Gay.
 *
 * Copyright (c) 1991, 2000, 2001 by Lucent Technologies.
 *
 * Permission to use, copy, modify, and distribute this software for any
 * purpose without fee is hereby granted, provided that this entire notice
 * is included in all copies of any software which is or includes a copy
 * or modification of this software and in all copies of the supporting
 * documentation for such software.
 *
 * THIS SOFTWARE IS BEING PROVIDED "AS IS", WITHOUT ANY EXPRESS OR IMPLIED
 * WARRANTY.  IN PARTICULAR, NEITHER THE AUTHOR NOR LUCENT MAKES ANY
 * REPRESENTATION OR WARRANTY OF ANY KIND CONCERNING THE MERCHANTABILITY
 * OF THIS SOFTWARE OR ITS FITNESS FOR ANY PARTICULAR PURPOSE.
 *
 **********************************************************************/
```

C.3.13 OpenSSL

The modules `hashlib`, `posix`, `ssl`, `crypt` use the OpenSSL library for added performance if made available by the operating system. Additionally, the Windows and Mac OS X installers for Python may include a copy of the OpenSSL libraries, so we include a copy of the OpenSSL license here:

```
LICENSE ISSUES
==============

The OpenSSL toolkit stays under a dual license, i.e. both the conditions of
the OpenSSL License and the original SSLeay license apply to the toolkit.
See below for the actual license texts. Actually both licenses are BSD-style
Open Source licenses. In case of any license issues related to OpenSSL
please contact openssl-core@openssl.org.

OpenSSL License
---------------

  /* ===================================================================
```

```
 * Copyright (c) 1998-2008 The OpenSSL Project.  All rights reserved.
 *
 * Redistribution and use in source and binary forms, with or without
 * modification, are permitted provided that the following conditions
 * are met:
 *
 * 1. Redistributions of source code must retain the above copyright
 *    notice, this list of conditions and the following disclaimer.
 *
 * 2. Redistributions in binary form must reproduce the above copyright
 *    notice, this list of conditions and the following disclaimer in
 *    the documentation and/or other materials provided with the
 *    distribution.
 *
 * 3. All advertising materials mentioning features or use of this
 *    software must display the following acknowledgment:
 *    "This product includes software developed by the OpenSSL Project
 *    for use in the OpenSSL Toolkit. (http://www.openssl.org/)"
 *
 * 4. The names "OpenSSL Toolkit" and "OpenSSL Project" must not be used to
 *    endorse or promote products derived from this software without
 *    prior written permission. For written permission, please contact
 *    openssl-core@openssl.org.
 *
 * 5. Products derived from this software may not be called "OpenSSL"
 *    nor may "OpenSSL" appear in their names without prior written
 *    permission of the OpenSSL Project.
 *
 * 6. Redistributions of any form whatsoever must retain the following
 *    acknowledgment:
 *    "This product includes software developed by the OpenSSL Project
 *    for use in the OpenSSL Toolkit (http://www.openssl.org/)"
 *
 * THIS SOFTWARE IS PROVIDED BY THE OpenSSL PROJECT ``AS IS'' AND ANY
 * EXPRESSED OR IMPLIED WARRANTIES, INCLUDING, BUT NOT LIMITED TO, THE
 * IMPLIED WARRANTIES OF MERCHANTABILITY AND FITNESS FOR A PARTICULAR
 * PURPOSE ARE DISCLAIMED.  IN NO EVENT SHALL THE OpenSSL PROJECT OR
 * ITS CONTRIBUTORS BE LIABLE FOR ANY DIRECT, INDIRECT, INCIDENTAL,
 * SPECIAL, EXEMPLARY, OR CONSEQUENTIAL DAMAGES (INCLUDING, BUT
 * NOT LIMITED TO, PROCUREMENT OF SUBSTITUTE GOODS OR SERVICES;
 * LOSS OF USE, DATA, OR PROFITS; OR BUSINESS INTERRUPTION)
 * HOWEVER CAUSED AND ON ANY THEORY OF LIABILITY, WHETHER IN CONTRACT,
 * STRICT LIABILITY, OR TORT (INCLUDING NEGLIGENCE OR OTHERWISE)
 * ARISING IN ANY WAY OUT OF THE USE OF THIS SOFTWARE, EVEN IF ADVISED
 * OF THE POSSIBILITY OF SUCH DAMAGE.
 * ======================================================================
 *
 * This product includes cryptographic software written by Eric Young
 * (eay@cryptsoft.com).  This product includes software written by Tim
 * Hudson (tjh@cryptsoft.com).
 *
 */
```

Original SSLeay License

```
----------------------
```

```
/* Copyright (C) 1995-1998 Eric Young (eay@cryptsoft.com)
 * All rights reserved.
 *
 * This package is an SSL implementation written
 * by Eric Young (eay@cryptsoft.com).
 * The implementation was written so as to conform with Netscapes SSL.
 *
 * This library is free for commercial and non-commercial use as long as
 * the following conditions are aheared to.  The following conditions
 * apply to all code found in this distribution, be it the RC4, RSA,
 * lhash, DES, etc., code; not just the SSL code.  The SSL documentation
 * included with this distribution is covered by the same copyright terms
 * except that the holder is Tim Hudson (tjh@cryptsoft.com).
 *
 * Copyright remains Eric Young's, and as such any Copyright notices in
 * the code are not to be removed.
 * If this package is used in a product, Eric Young should be given attribution
 * as the author of the parts of the library used.
 * This can be in the form of a textual message at program startup or
 * in documentation (online or textual) provided with the package.
 *
 * Redistribution and use in source and binary forms, with or without
 * modification, are permitted provided that the following conditions
 * are met:
 * 1. Redistributions of source code must retain the copyright
 *    notice, this list of conditions and the following disclaimer.
 * 2. Redistributions in binary form must reproduce the above copyright
 *    notice, this list of conditions and the following disclaimer in the
 *    documentation and/or other materials provided with the distribution.
 * 3. All advertising materials mentioning features or use of this software
 *    must display the following acknowledgement:
 *    "This product includes cryptographic software written by
 *     Eric Young (eay@cryptsoft.com)"
 *    The word 'cryptographic' can be left out if the rouines from the library
 *    being used are not cryptographic related :-).
 * 4. If you include any Windows specific code (or a derivative thereof) from
 *    the apps directory (application code) you must include an acknowledgement:
 *    "This product includes software written by Tim Hudson (tjh@cryptsoft.com)"
 *
 * THIS SOFTWARE IS PROVIDED BY ERIC YOUNG ``AS IS'' AND
 * ANY EXPRESS OR IMPLIED WARRANTIES, INCLUDING, BUT NOT LIMITED TO, THE
 * IMPLIED WARRANTIES OF MERCHANTABILITY AND FITNESS FOR A PARTICULAR PURPOSE
 * ARE DISCLAIMED.  IN NO EVENT SHALL THE AUTHOR OR CONTRIBUTORS BE LIABLE
 * FOR ANY DIRECT, INDIRECT, INCIDENTAL, SPECIAL, EXEMPLARY, OR CONSEQUENTIAL
 * DAMAGES (INCLUDING, BUT NOT LIMITED TO, PROCUREMENT OF SUBSTITUTE GOODS
 * OR SERVICES; LOSS OF USE, DATA, OR PROFITS; OR BUSINESS INTERRUPTION)
 * HOWEVER CAUSED AND ON ANY THEORY OF LIABILITY, WHETHER IN CONTRACT, STRICT
 * LIABILITY, OR TORT (INCLUDING NEGLIGENCE OR OTHERWISE) ARISING IN ANY WAY
 * OUT OF THE USE OF THIS SOFTWARE, EVEN IF ADVISED OF THE POSSIBILITY OF
 * SUCH DAMAGE.
 *
 * The licence and distribution terms for any publically available version or
```

```
 * derivative of this code cannot be changed.  i.e. this code cannot simply be
 * copied and put under another distribution licence
 * [including the GNU Public Licence.]
 */
```

C.3.14 expat

The `pyexpat` extension is built using an included copy of the expat sources unless the build is configured `--with-system-expat`:

```
Copyright (c) 1998, 1999, 2000 Thai Open Source Software Center Ltd
                         and Clark Cooper

Permission is hereby granted, free of charge, to any person obtaining
a copy of this software and associated documentation files (the
"Software"), to deal in the Software without restriction, including
without limitation the rights to use, copy, modify, merge, publish,
distribute, sublicense, and/or sell copies of the Software, and to
permit persons to whom the Software is furnished to do so, subject to
the following conditions:

The above copyright notice and this permission notice shall be included
in all copies or substantial portions of the Software.

THE SOFTWARE IS PROVIDED "AS IS", WITHOUT WARRANTY OF ANY KIND,
EXPRESS OR IMPLIED, INCLUDING BUT NOT LIMITED TO THE WARRANTIES OF
MERCHANTABILITY, FITNESS FOR A PARTICULAR PURPOSE AND NONINFRINGEMENT.
IN NO EVENT SHALL THE AUTHORS OR COPYRIGHT HOLDERS BE LIABLE FOR ANY
CLAIM, DAMAGES OR OTHER LIABILITY, WHETHER IN AN ACTION OF CONTRACT,
TORT OR OTHERWISE, ARISING FROM, OUT OF OR IN CONNECTION WITH THE
SOFTWARE OR THE USE OR OTHER DEALINGS IN THE SOFTWARE.
```

C.3.15 libffi

The `_ctypes` extension is built using an included copy of the libffi sources unless the build is configured `--with-system-libffi`:

```
Copyright (c) 1996-2008  Red Hat, Inc and others.

Permission is hereby granted, free of charge, to any person obtaining
a copy of this software and associated documentation files (the
``Software''), to deal in the Software without restriction, including
without limitation the rights to use, copy, modify, merge, publish,
distribute, sublicense, and/or sell copies of the Software, and to
permit persons to whom the Software is furnished to do so, subject to
the following conditions:

The above copyright notice and this permission notice shall be included
in all copies or substantial portions of the Software.

THE SOFTWARE IS PROVIDED ``AS IS'', WITHOUT WARRANTY OF ANY KIND,
EXPRESS OR IMPLIED, INCLUDING BUT NOT LIMITED TO THE WARRANTIES OF
MERCHANTABILITY, FITNESS FOR A PARTICULAR PURPOSE AND
```

```
NONINFRINGEMENT.  IN NO EVENT SHALL THE AUTHORS OR COPYRIGHT
HOLDERS BE LIABLE FOR ANY CLAIM, DAMAGES OR OTHER LIABILITY,
WHETHER IN AN ACTION OF CONTRACT, TORT OR OTHERWISE, ARISING FROM,
OUT OF OR IN CONNECTION WITH THE SOFTWARE OR THE USE OR OTHER
DEALINGS IN THE SOFTWARE.
```

C.3.16 zlib

The `zlib` extension is built using an included copy of the zlib sources if the zlib version found on the system is too old to be used for the build:

```
Copyright (C) 1995-2010 Jean-loup Gailly and Mark Adler

This software is provided 'as-is', without any express or implied
warranty.  In no event will the authors be held liable for any damages
arising from the use of this software.

Permission is granted to anyone to use this software for any purpose,
including commercial applications, and to alter it and redistribute it
freely, subject to the following restrictions:

1. The origin of this software must not be misrepresented; you must not
   claim that you wrote the original software. If you use this software
   in a product, an acknowledgment in the product documentation would be
   appreciated but is not required.

2. Altered source versions must be plainly marked as such, and must not be
   misrepresented as being the original software.

3. This notice may not be removed or altered from any source distribution.

Jean-loup Gailly        Mark Adler
jloup@gzip.org          madler@alumni.caltech.edu
```

COPYRIGHT

Python and this documentation is:

See *History and License* for complete license and permissions information.